Deviance and the Family

The *Marriage & Family Review* series:

- *Family Medicine: A New Approach to Health Care*, edited by Betty E. Cogswell and Marvin B. Sussman

- *Cults and the Family*, edited by Florence Kaslow and Marvin B. Sussman

- *Alternatives to Traditional Family Living*, edited by Harriet Gross and Marvin B. Sussman

- *Intermarriage in the United States*, edited by Gary A. Crester and Joseph J. Leon

- *Family Systems and Inheritance Patterns*, edited by Judith N. Cates and Marvin B. Sussman

- *The Ties that Bind: Men's and Women's Social Networks*, edited by Laura Lein and Marvin B. Sussman

- *Social Stress and the Family: Advances and Developments in Family Stress Theory and Research*, edited by Hamilton I. McCubbin, Marvin B. Sussman, and Joan M. Patterson

- *Human Sexuality and the Family*, edited by James W. Maddock, Gerhard Neubeck, and Marvin B. Sussman

- *Obesity and the Family*, edited by David J. Kallen and Marvin B. Sussman

- *Women and the Family*, edited by Beth B. Hess and Marvin B. Sussman

- *Personal Computers and the Family*, edited by Marvin B. Sussman

- *Pets and the Family*, edited by Marvin B. Sussman

- *Families and the Energy Transition*, edited by John Byrne, David A. Schulz, and Marvin B. Sussman

- *Men's Changing Roles in the Family*, edited by Robert A. Lewis and Marvin B. Sussman

- *The Charybdis Complex: Redemption of Rejected Marriage and Family Journal Articles*, edited by Marvin B. Sussman

- *Families and the Prospect of Nuclear Attack/Holocaust*, edited by Teresa D. Marciano and Marvin B. Sussman

- *Family Medicine: The Maturing of a Discipline*, edited by William J. Doherty, Charles E. Christianson, and Marvin B. Sussman

- *Childhood Disability and Family Systems*, edited by Michael Ferrari and Marvin B. Sussman

- *Alternative Health Maintenance and Healing Systems for Families*, edited by Doris Y. Wilkinson and Marvin B. Sussman

- *Deviance and the Family*, edited by Frank E. Hagan and Marvin B. Sussman

Deviance and the Family

Frank E. Hagan
Marvin B. Sussman
Editors

The Haworth Press
New York • London

Deviance and the Family has also been published as *Marriage & Family Review,* Volume 12, Numbers 1/2 1987.

The Haworth Press, Inc., 12 West 32 Street, New York, NY 10001
EUROSPAN/Haworth, 3 Henrietta Street, London WC2E 8LU England

LIBRARY OF CONGRESS
Library of Congress Cataloging-in-Publication Data

Deviance and the family/Frank E. Hagan, Marvin B. Sussman, editors.
   p. cm
  ISBN 0-86656-726-7
  1. Family—United States. 2. Deviant behavior. 3. Family violence—United States.
  4. Juvenile delinquency—United States.
 I. Hagan, Frank E. II. Sussman, Marvin B.
HQ536.D44 1988
362.8'2—dc19
                                               87-34244
                                               CIP

Deviance and the Family

CONTENTS

Deviance and the Family: Where Have We Been and Where Are We Going?

Frank E. Hagan
Marvin B. Sussman

INTRODUCTION

Deviant behavior refers to a broad range of activities which society, especially those who are in power, views as eccentric, dangerous, annoying, bizarre, outlandish, gross, abhorrent or criminal. It refers to behavior which is outside the range of normal toleration. The range of this toleration and thus the definitions of deviance are relative to time, place, and person(s) making the evaluation. Crime and delinquency are among the types of deviant behavior which will be examined in this paper. Crime refers specifically to activities which violate criminal law. While including criminal acts, delinquency particularly in the United States includes a variety of activities which would not be considered criminal if committed by an adult. Curfew violations, incorrigibility and truancy are examples. Thus, crime and delinquency and most other forms of social deviance are socially defined behaviors rather than given biomedical conditions. This fact will have much bearing in examining theoretical attempts to explain deviance causation as well as the role of the family in the deviance and criminal activities of its members.

There is a current myth that crime starts in the home by parents

Frank E. Hagan is Professor of Sociology and Criminal Justice and Director, Graduate Program in Criminal Justice Administration, Mercyhurst College, 501 E. 38 Street, Glenwood Hills, Erie, PA 16546. Marvin B. Sussman is Unidel Professor of Human Behavior, College of Human Resources, University of Delaware, Newark, DE 19716.

1

who imperfectly socialize their children. Thus it is the parents' fault if a child goes wrong. While the family plays an important role in the socialization process and family characteristics and conditions do predispose some family members to delinquent and criminal careers, these assumptions are gross oversimplifications of a more complex reality.

In recent years attention has been focused upon the family and its role in the causes of delinquency. Many American studies of delinquency include activities such as truancy and incorrigibility that are not considered criminal if committed by an adult. Reviews of family factors associated with delinquency (Sutherland & Cressey, 1974: 203-218; Hirschi, 1983: 53-68) point to moderate-to-high correlations with immorality, criminality or alcoholism of parents, absence of one or both parents, lack of parental control, unhappy home life, subcultural differences in the home and economic pressures. Family influences also relate to the fact that parental social class determines the residence, school and associates of their offspring. Family transmission of criminogenic attitudes or failure to train the child may influence delinquency while a poor home environment may force youth into the streets seeking peer group support (Hagan, 1986: 83).

CRIMINOLOGICAL THEORY AND THE FAMILY

Theoretical analysis of the family as a factor in deviance or crime causation finds the family as a variable which may or may not play a role in larger theoretical schemes. Figure 1 identifies major theoretical approaches in criminology and indicates if the family is considered to be a critical variable by each school.

The very earliest theories of crime were *demonological* or supernatural explanations. These dominated thinking from early history well into the 18th century and still have modern remnants. In a system of knowledge in which theological explanations of reality were predominant, the criminal was viewed as a sinner who was possessed by demons or damned by otherworldly forces. The family was not a critical factor in this supernatural paradigm.

Primary challenge to theological approaches explaining reality would be philosophical. Worldly, rational and secular explanations

FIGURE 1 -- MAJOR THEORETICAL APPROACHES IN CRIMINOLOGY*

Theoretical School	Major Themes/Concepts	Major Theorists	Family as Critical Variable
Demonological	criminal as "evil," "sinner," "supernatural pawn"	traditional authority	No
Classical (Neo-Classical)	criminal as "rational, hedonistic, free actor" "incapacitation, punishment, deterrence"	Beccaria, Bentham Wilson, G. Becker	No
Ecological (Geographic)	"group characteristics, physical and social ecological impacts upon criminality" "geographical and climatic impacts upon criminality"	Quetelet & Guerry Lieber & Sherin	No
Economic	"capitalism, social class inequality and economic conditions cause crime"	Marx, Bonger	No
Positivistic Biological	"physical stigmata, atavism, biological inheritance causes criminality" "mental deficiency" "feeblemindedness" "physical inferiority" "somatotypes-mesomorphs" "brain disorders, twin studies, XYY syndrome, physiological disorders"	Lombroso, Ferri, Garofalo Goring Goddard Hooton Sheldon Moniz, Christiansen, Jacobs	Yes
Psychological	"unconscious repression of sexual instincts," "criminal personality," "extroversion," "inadequate behavioral conditioning," "IQ"	Freud, Eysenck, Skinner, Hirschi, Hindelang	Yes

FIGURE 1 -- MAJOR THEORETICAL APPROACHES IN CRIMINOLOGY (SOCIOLOGICAL)

Theoretical School	Major Themes/Concepts	Major Theorists	Family as Critical Variable
Sociological Mainstream	"crime reflects consensus model"		
Anomie Theory	"anomie (normlessness) lessens social control" "anomie (gap between goals and means) creates deviance" "differential social opportunity" "lower class reaction to middle class values"	Durkheim Merton Cloward and Ohlin Cohen	No
Social Process	"crime is learned behavior, culturally/ subculturally transmitted" "social disorganization and social conditions" "focal concerns of lower class" "subterranean values, drift, techniques of neutralization"	Sutherland Shaw and McKay Miller Matza	Yes
Social Control	"social bonds weakened reducing individual stakes in conformity" "containment theory"	Hirschi Reckless	Yes
Critical	"crime reflects conflict model"		
Labeling	"societal reaction theory" "dramatization of evil" "secondary deviance" "crime as label, status"	Tannenbaum Lemert	No
Conflict	"pluralistic model" "more powerful groups define criminal law" "imperatively coordinated associations"	Vold Turk Dahrendorf	No
Radical	"neo-Marxist"; "capitalism causes crime"	Chambliss, Quinney	No

* Source: Portions adapted from Frank E. Hagan, Introduction to Criminology: Theories, Methods and Criminal Behavior, Chicago: Nelson-Hall, 1986, 392, 432.

4

were made for human fate. The reasons for crime and criminality are found not in the supernatural, but the natural world.

Italian Cesare Beccaria (1738-1794) along with British philosopher Jeremy Bentham (1748-1832) were the principal advocates of the *classical school of criminology*. They viewed individuals acting as a result of "free will" and motivated by hedonism, the seeking of pleasure and avoidance of pain. All persons were perceived as maximizers of pleasure including deviant or criminal ones until the anticipated pain outweighed the anticipated pleasure. Advocating rational explanations, this school focused attention on criminal law rather than behavior with emphasis upon the acts of individuals rather than groups such as the family. While revivals of neoclassical theory admit environmental, psychological and other mitigating circumstances as modifying conditions to classical doctrine, they do not focus upon the family as having a critical role in influencing deviant behavior of family members.

The two main adherents of the *ecological school* of criminological theory were Belgian Adolphe Quetelet (1796-1874) and Frenchman A. M. Guerry (1802-1866). Sometimes called the statistical, geographic or cartographic school, these writers emphasized group factors and characteristics and their impact upon crime. While concentrating upon such sociological characteristics as climate, heterogeneity of population and poverty, Quetelet and Guerry did not particularly address the issue of the family as a factor in crime.

The inspirational figure behind most *economic criminological theories* was Karl Marx (1818-1883) who insisted that the economic substructure determines the nature of all other institutions and social relationships in society. The family was not a critical entity in Marxian theory or in the works of a foremost early Marxist criminologist, Dutch philosopher Willem Bonger (1876-1940). In his *Criminality and Economic Conditions* (Bonger, 1969), published in 1910, Bonger emphasized inequality and capitalism as the primary causes of criminal behavior. A major shift in unit of analysis in criminology would be heralded, however, with the emergence and ascendancy of *positivism*. Stressing a scientific approach, positivists were interested in explaining and treating individual pathology. Deviation from group norms was viewed as a weakness or sickness of the individual.

EARLY BIOLOGICAL
AND PSYCHOLOGICAL POSITIVISM

The origins of *biological positivism* can be traced to the writings of Cesare Lombroso (1835-1909) as well as his disciples Enrico Ferri (1856-1929) and Raffaelo Garofalo (1852-1934). In his early writings Lombroso (1911) was heavily influenced by Darwin's theory of evolution which led him to emphasize the notion of "born criminals." Such individuals were viewed as "atavistic" throwbacks to an earlier and more primitive evolutionary period and could be noted by certain "physical stigmata," outward appearances, particulary facial, which distinguished them from noncriminals. Such early positivists used poor sampling techniques, their findings were statistically insignificant and ignored the fact that physical stigmata were most likely environmentally induced defects due to poverty and malnutrition rather than inherited genetically. Charles Goring (1870-1919) proposed inherited mental defectiveness as a cause of criminality (Goring, 1913) evidenced by two classic family case studies: the Jukes and the Kallikaks.

Published only a year after Lombroso's *Criminal Man*, Robert Dugdale's (1841-1883) *The Jukes* (1877) was a case study of generations of an American family. Tracing over 1,000 descendants of Ada Jukes (a pseudonym), he found 280 paupers, 60 thieves, 7 murderers, 140 criminals, 40 venereal disease victims, 50 prostitutes, as well as other various deviants—proof positive, he claimed, of inherited criminality. Henry Goddard (1912) conducted a similar study entitled *The Kallikak Family*, an analysis of the offspring of one Martin Kallikak, a militiaman during the American Revolutionary War. Kallikak fathered a child out of wedlock to a "feebleminded barwench" and a large number of descendants of this union were feebleminded, or deviant. The offspring of his marriage to a "respectable" woman were, on the other hand, all of the highest moral and mental standards. Goddard took these findings as proof positive of feeblemindedness (low mentality) as the cause of crime. Another neo-Lombrosian, Earnest Hooton (1887-1954) claimed on the basis of a very detailed and extensive study of physical differences between criminals and noncriminals that he had discovered the cause of criminality: physical inferiority.

Some *common problems* shared by these early biological positiv-

istic theories included the mistaken assumption that one could genetically inherit a trait or propensity (to violate criminal laws)
which is socially defined and culturally relative. Ignoring social and
cultural factors, the biopositivists share a conservative consensus
world view, an unquestioned acceptance of official definitions of
crime and the social class bias that crime is primarily to be found
among "the dangerous classes." Most of these studies reflect the
"dualistic fallacy" (Reid, 1982: 657) which assumes the mutual
exclusivity of criminals (defined as prisoners) and noncriminals
(defined as nonprisoners). Most of their analyses are plagued by
weak operationalization or measurement of key concepts such as
"feebleminded," "inferior" and "crime." Modern genetics has
discredited most of these simplistic theories and speaks against notions of inheritance of acquired characteristics, emphasizing instead
selective adaptation and mutation (Vold, 1979: 100).

For these reasons modern criminology has largely abandoned biological or genetic familial aspects of crime causation until recently. Sagarin (1980) views the exploration of many of these subject areas as unfortunately representing *Taboos in Criminology*,
topics which have been viewed as "untouchable," "fruitless" or
"mined-out." Van den Berghe (1974) in an article entitled "Bringing the Beasts Back In" argued that modern criminology, in rejecting early positivism, had swung the other way and was ignoring the
biological basis of human behavior. Shah and Roth (1974) in a review of criminology's "nature-nurture" controversy (whether
criminality is explained by genetics or environment) detail a variety
of research including biochemical effects, brain disorders, endo-
crine and hormonal problems, nerve disorders and other factors
which can hardly be ignored at least in explaining individual cases
of criminality. Illustrative of their point are twin and adoption studies which are ingenious ways of attempting to address the "nature
vs. nurture" debate, that is, whether criminality is inherited or
learned.

Twin/Adoption Studies

Ex post facto in nature, twin studies begin with criminals who
have a twin and then attempt to find the other in order to discover
whether he or she is also criminal (Lange, 1931; Rosanoff, Handy &

Plesset, 1934; Christiansen, 1968; Dalgard & Kringlen, 1975). Such studies often compare monozygotic (MZ) with dizygotic (DZ) twins. Monozygotic (identical) twins since they are produced by a single egg exhibit the same hereditary environment, while dizygotic (fraternal) twins portray less biological similarity being the product of separate eggs.

Despite painstaking research and admirable scholarship, the findings of twin studies have been mixed. Dalgard and Kringlen's (Ibid.) study of all twins born in Norway between 1900 and 1935 concluded that the significance of hereditary factors in registered crime was nonexistent. Out of 33,000 twins, 139 twins were found where one or the other had been known to have committed a crime. Their study and others found greater concordance (similar criminal behavior) among MZ twins than among DZ twins. Mednick and Volavka (1980) in a review of studies from 1929 to 1961 found roughly 60% concordance among MZs and 30% among DZ pairs, while Christiansen's (1968) research of 3,586 male twins found 52% MZ concordance and 22% among DZs.

Adoption studies assume that, if the behavior of children more closely matches that of their biological parents than that of their adoptive parents, then greater support would be lent to the biological basis of human behavior. Schulsinger (1972) found criminality in adopted boys to be higher if their biological fathers had criminal records. In a study of 1,145 male adoptees born in Copenhagen between 1927 and 1941, Hutchings and Mednick (1977) found 185 adoptees with criminal records with criminality of biological father a major predictor. Crowe (1974) found no differences between adoptees and a control group, although the former exhibited a higher proportion of psychopathic personalities. He admits, however, that environmental differences may have been responsible for this finding as well as problems with a small sample.

Most twin and adoption studies involve a small number of cases because they attempt to examine two rare events: twins/adoptees and crime. A shift of only a few cases which may have been misdiagnosed can erase the claimed MZ-DZ differences. Even if higher concordance is found among MZs this may be due to more similar environmental treatment in which identical twins are more likely to be treated the same.

XYY Syndrome

In the late 1950s in England speculation began regarding males who possessed an XYY chromosome pattern — an extra male chromosome. Of the 46 chromosomes humans possess, males receive an X chromosome from their mothers and a Y chromosome from their fathers, while females receive two X chromosomes, one from each parent. Beginning with studies by Patricia Jacobs et al. (1965), in which a large number of Scottish inmates were found to be "double Ys," the hypothesis had been proposed of the existence of a "double male" or "supermale syndrome." Such males were variously described as unusually tall, to have suffered severe acne in childhood and to be predisposed to aggressive and violent behavior.

While early research suggested that prisoners were disproportionately "double Ys," further research found no greater proportions than is to be expected in the general population (Shah & Roth, 1974: 137; Witkin et al., 1976). A Danish study by Witkin et al. (Ibid.) did not support the aggression hypothesis and found that incarcerated XYYs showed less aggression while in prison than did the other inmates. Earlier reviews of the research by Fox (1971) and Sarbin and Miller (1970) essentially agreed with these findings and found XYYs when institutionalized to have less serious offense records than others. Ellis' (1982) review of the XYY literature provides inconclusive findings. While more research is needed, negative findings have considerably lessened interest in the XYY syndrome as a cause of criminality.

Psychological Positivism

Various psychological, psychiatric and psychoanalytic theories of criminality share in common the search for individual criminal pathology in the human personality. Many adherents of this approach concentrate more on applied therapy and rehabilitation of identified criminals and less on theoretical explanations of causation. The intellectual forefather to these approaches was Sigmund Freud (1856-1939). Although he did not address his writings to the crime issue, his theories of personality and psychopathology have been applied to explanations of criminal and deviant behavior, particularly mental illness.

The family and its socialization function was central to Freudian explanation. Psychoanalytic adherents of Freudian theory view much criminality as being unconsciously motivated and often due to the repression (hiding or sublimation into the unconscious) of personality conflicts and unresolved problems experienced in early childhood and the family socialization process. Relying extensively upon case studies, Freudians document examples of the Oedipus or Electra complex, the death wish, inferiority complex, frustration-aggression, birth trauma, castration fears and penis envy, in which crime is a substitute for forbidden acts (Vold & Bernard, 1986: 111-117).

Attempts to measure psychological and mental differences between criminals and noncriminals have been unable to conclusively turn up specific personality characteristics related to criminality (Schuessler & Cressey, 1953; Waldo & Dinitz, 1967; Tennenbaum, 1977). Hirschi and Hindelang (1977), however, point to a rather consistent deficit in IQ on the part of delinquents with race and social class controlled.

Yochelson and Samenow (1976) claim that on the basis of therapeutic work with 240 hard-core criminals and delinquent subjects they discovered a "criminal personality" and that socioenvironmental constraints on individual criminality are irrelevant. This criminal personality is imprinted at birth and relatively unaffected by the family. Yochelson and Samenow fail to cite any convincing empirical evidence and they fail to refute evidence regarding environmental and social influences.

The state of the "nature versus nurture debate" can best be summed up by Monahan and Splane (1980: 42): "What the field of criminology needs, it appears to us, are sociologists who use psychological intervening variables without embarrassment and psychologists who are aware of the social roots of the individual processes they study."

Sociological Approaches

The sociological approaches to criminology are quite diverse. Research with respect to the family has concentrated upon juvenile delinquency. Most of the newer perspectives in criminological theory were the product of sociological thought which focused attention upon social categories rather than upon individuals. Wilson and Herrnstein (1985: 215) state that in the 1950s the study of the family severed its connections with criminological matters. Hirschi (1983: 54) corroborates this point: "The major reason for the neglect of the family is that explanations of crime that focus on the family are directly contrary to the metaphysics of our age . . . They assume that the individual would not be criminal were it not for the operation of unjust and misguided institutions."

The sociological approaches to criminal theory are depicted in Figure 1 and consist of mainstream approaches (anomie, social process and social control) and critical approaches (labeling, conflict and radical).

Anomie theories originate in the writings of French sociologist Emile Durkheim (1858-1917). Anomie describes a moral malaise; a lack of clear-cut norms with which to guide human conduct; a state of normlessness. The close ties of the individual to the family, village and tradition (what Durkheim called "mechanical solidarity") weakens in modern society and these constraints are replaced by individualism and associational bonds ("organic solidarity") (Durkheim, 1951). This notion of anomie would influence a number of sociologists most notably Robert Merton, Richard Cloward and Lloyd Ohlin and Albert Cohen. All focused upon larger social processes and not particularly upon the family as an important factor in deviance. For Merton (1961) discrepancies between societal goals and adequate means for their achievement generated anti-social behavior, while Cloward and Ohlin (1960) suggest differential social opportunity and availability of legitimate and illegitimate criminal opportunities. The gang, peer group, neighborhood and larger society were implicitly viewed as more important in this process than the family. Cohen (1955) viewed delinquency as a lower class reaction to unobtainable middle class values. These writers failed to address in detail the family as a critical variable (Bordua, 1962).

Social process theories emphasize criminality as a learned or culturally transmitted process and are represented as an outgrowth of the "Chicago school of sociology" in the works of Henry Shaw, David McKay, Edwin Sutherland, Walter Miller, and David Matza.

The Chicago school, begun in 1892, was the first academic program in sociology in the United States. Urban ecology, viewing the city as a natural organism and its differentiation into "natural areas," ones which serve specialized functions, e.g., a "zone of transition," an interstitial area which bred social disorganization, was its predominant theme (Stein, 1964). Shaw and McKay based their ecological studies in the 1930s on the basic premise that crime is due more to social disorganization in pathological environments than it is to abnormal individuals committing deviant behavior (Gibbons, 1979: 45).

Perhaps the most influential general theory of criminality, differential association, was proposed initially in 1934 by Edwin Sutherland (1883-1950). Individuals become predisposed toward criminality due to an excess of contacts which advocate criminal behavior. A person will learn and accept values and attitudes which look more favorably upon criminality from such repetitive contacts. Sutherland's theory emphasizes that the learning of criminal behavior occurs in intimate personal groups and that the family can transmit criminal values directly to offspring. His theory, however, did not elaborate on any special role played by the family (Sutherland & Cressey, 1974).

Walter Miller (1958) viewed criminality as reflecting the focal concerns of lower class subcultures. He assumes the existence of a distinctive lower class subculture which holds values and attitudes at odds with dominant middle class values. Thus social class rather than family becomes the predominant unit of analysis.

The theories of David Matza (1964) and with his colleague Gresham Sykes (Matza & Sykes, 1961) emphasize the delinquent as drifting between criminal and conventional action. The delinquent acts out "subterranean values" of society, underground or illicit values which exist side by side with more conventional ones. Delinquents utilize rationalizations or "techniques of neutralization" to explain away personal responsibility for their actions. One means of denial of responsibility is an appeal based upon one's poor home life, lack of affection and social class. Matza's theories while only touching upon the family as a variable provides a transition to social control theories with his notion of drift, in which individuals become temporarily detached from social control mechanisms.

Social control theories emphasize the release from social bonds as the basic unit of analysis. Represented in the writings of Walter Reckless and Travis Hirschi among others, social control theories address the issue of how society maintains or elicits social control and how it obtains conformity or fails to obtain it in the form of deviance. Reckless' (1961) containment theory holds that individuals have various social controls (containments) which assist them in resisting pressures which draw them toward criminality. The presence or absence of social pressures interacts with the presence or absence of containments to produce or not produce individual criminality. A major containment is represented by an effective family and near support systems which assist in reinforcing conventionality and insulating the individual from the assault of outside pressures. Individuals may become predisposed toward criminality due to strong external pressures and pulls and weak inner and outer containments, while others with these same pressures may resist due to a strong family or through a strong sense of self. While actual empirical specification of containment theory has been problematic (Reckless, Dinitz & Murray, 1956; Scarpitti et al. 1960; Schrag, 1971) the containment theory has proved a very useful descriptive model which subsumes many variables discussed in more specific theories.

The most influential theory in the social control tradition is Hirschi's (1969) social bond theory. Delinquency is viewed as taking place when a person's bonds to society are broken or weakened thus reducing his or her stakes in conformity. The fear of rupturing relationships with family, friends, neighbors, jobs and schools and the image such groups hold of the person keeps one in line. These bonds consist of *attachment*, bonds to others such as family; *commitment*, a vested interest in the social and economic system; *involvement*, engagement in legitimate social activities; and *belief* in conventional values and norms. Social bond theory has also been well received due to its ability as a general theory to take into account many more particularistic theories.

Critical criminological theory consists of three major types of approaches: the labeling perspective, conflict theory and the radical (Marxist) viewpoint. Represented by writers such as Lemert

(1967), Turk (1969) and Quinney (1974) critical theorists were concerned with wider level societal relationships, ignoring the family as a critical explanatory variable. Some of their basic assumptions are that crime is a label attached to behavior, usually of the less powerful in society. More powerful groups control the labeling process in order to protect their basic interests. They assume that the conflict model rather than consensus model explains the criminalization process and crime is often a rational response to inequitable conditions in capitalistic societies.

FAMILY STUDIES AND CRIMINALITY

Review of criminological theoretical approaches with respect to inclusion of the family as a critical variable suggests that only the positivistic, social process and social control theories include the family as a primary factor. The earliest studies which concentrated upon heredity and crime were described as suffering from severe methodological difficulties and are regarded today as little more than curious historical footnotes.

More sophisticated family studies of delinquents could be noted with research by Sheldon and Eleanor Glueck (1951) who examined 500 delinquents and 500 nondelinquents and found roughly 50% of delinquents were from broken homes compared with about 29% of nondelinquents. Delinquents were more likely to have families characterized by physical illness, mental retardation, mental disturbance, alcoholism and parental criminality. Such parents exercised poor child rearing practices, either overly strict or overly permissive and inconsistent. Thus defective family relations was perceived as a key causal variable in delinquency.

The longest longitudinal study of delinquents, the Cambridge-Somerville study, was begun in 1937. Six hundred and fifty boys (average age of 11) were selected for in-depth study. William and Joan McCord (1955) in analyzing these data found that delinquents were characterized by poor or weak parental discipline as well as a quarrelsome home environment. The McCords found that family structure, broken or intact home, was less salient than the nature of family interaction. All of the boys from quarrelsome environments had been convicted of crime (Wilson & Herrnstein, 1985: 232).

West and Farrington (1973) undertook a longitudinal study of 411 London working class boys for 17 years beginning at age eight. By age 25, 30 of the sample had committed over half of the recorded convictions. Factors associated with delinquency included: low IQ, poor child rearing practices, criminality of father, large family size and low family income. Similar findings with respect to defective parental supervision and socialization have been suggested by Hirschi (1969), Baumrind (1978), and Patterson (1982). Advocates of family systems theory and family therapy (Minuchin et al., 1967; Satir, 1974) have long suggested that delinquency or deviance on the part of an adolescent is merely a "presenting problem"—a symptom of deeper, more underlying disruption within the family system as a whole. The entire family becomes the "patient" or "rehabilitation client."

A continual subject of debate in examining the family and delinquency is the broken home. Toby (1957) found broken homes associated with delinquency particularly for girls and younger boys, while Datesman and Scarpitti (1976) found this association for girls was primarily for status offenses, juvenile offenses which would not be considered criminal had they been committed by an adult. Contradictions in the research findings abound with many studies showing a broken home effect (Wilson & Herrnstein, 1985: 246), but just as many showing no impact (McCord & McCord, 1955; Robins, 1966; Hirschi, 1969).

The effect of broken homes obviously interacts with other variables and differs depending upon context, loss of parent through death has a different impact than if through divorce. Unhappy or discordant homes appear to produce greater delinquency than simply broken ones (McCord & McCord, 1959: 64; Nye, 1958). Wilson and Herrnstein (1985: 261) conclude their review of the literature by indicating that "a broken or abusive home is only an imperfect indicator of the existence of a complex array of factors that contribute to criminality."

Elliott Currie (1985: 183-184) has correctly indicated that interest in the relationship between the family and delinquency reflects broader ideological trends in society rather than the fruits of any new research breakthroughs. Conservative writers who have more recently dominated the literature, such as Hirschi (1983) and

Wilson and Herrnstein (1985), often view material disadvantage and quality of family life as mutually exclusive explanations. Currie calls this belief, that what goes on in the family is somehow separate from outside social forces that affect the family, the "fallacy of autonomy" (Currie, 1985: 185). These conservatives fail to view the family in a larger social context, have an obsessive concern with control rather than supportive social policies and lend the impression of intractability of family problems, unresponsive to enlightened social policy.

A long recognized limitation of many, particularly early, discussions of crime as well as theories of crime causation relates to the loose manner in which the definition of crime is employed and units of analysis are studied. The only thing most crimes have in common is that they are defined as violations of criminal law. Methodologists have long recognized invalidities introduced in research findings due to confusion in units of analysis. Robinson (1950) speaks of an "ecological fallacy" with which to refer to the error of drawing conclusions regarding individual behavior on the basis of data which have been derived from group or areal statistics.

In criminological theory a theoretical counterpart can be found in what might be described as the "global fallacy," a tendency to attempt to generalize relatively specific explanations to all types of crimes. Many individual theories are not invalid in themselves, but are either too globally ambitious or interpreted as such (Hagan, 1985). Analysis of crime within the family may concentrate upon nonviolent and violent crime, parental child stealing and marital rape. Crime by the family may examine the familial transmission of crime, while the family may also be a victim of crime (Lincoln & Straus, 1985). The impact of the family will vary with the type of criminal behavior being examined: violent, public order, conventional or occasional property, occupational, corporate, political, organized or professional.

The papers in this volume explore the myriad relationships between the family and specific forms of deviance and reflect an interdisciplinary approach by including works by practitioners as well as by academic researchers. Patricia R. Koski in "Family Violence and Nonfamily Deviance: Taking Stock of the Literature" indicates that despite research interest in this relationship many questions still remain unanswered. Her review of the literature concludes that much of the research remains largely descriptive and piecemeal. One obvious conclusion is that unhealthy families tend to produce deviant children in unexpected ways.

Tapping the growing literature and theories on intrafamily violence, Peter C. Kratcoski in "Families Who Kill" empirically explores this phenomenon. Noting that homicide is a crime which predominantly involves family members, friends or close acquaintances, he utilizes stress, systems, exchange/social control and social learning theories of family violence as a basis for inquiry. Kratcoski characterizes such homicides as often a crisis situation response to some family occurrence or catharsis of built-up anger over behavior of the family member-victim.

"The Criminalization of Forced Marital Intercourse" is examined by Robert T. Sigler and Donna Haygood. Their public opinion survey conducted in Tuscaloosa, Alabama, finds over half of their sample endorsing the criminalization of forced marital intercourse. Beginning with the 1978 *State vs. Rideout* case in Oregon in which "marital immunity" was challenged by the state, Sigler and Haygood discuss the changing societal orientation toward sex roles with major redefinition of the roles of women and the characteristics of societal response and obligation toward women.

Noting that police intervention in domestic affairs has been a subject of extensive commentary, but limited research, Daniel J. Bell empirically explores this relationship in "The Victim-Offender Relationship: A Determinant Factor in Police Domestic Dispute Dispositions." He finds wives to be the predominant victims and that in two-thirds of the reported incidents no official action is taken by the police—indirectly condoning husbands assaulting their wives. Only about one-quarter of incidents reported to the police result in criminal complaints being issued and only 16% result in arrests. While the highest incidence of arrests are recorded when wives initiate criminal complaints, there is little help from the police unless the wife files a complaint.

Michael W. H. Len in "Parental Discipline and Criminal Deviance" provides an ex post facto examination of prisoners' attitudes toward their parental discipline as children. His findings contradict claims of Yochelson and Samenow who claim that "parent-blaming" is a major rationalization employed by prisoners. Len finds that the prisoners interviewed took personal responsibility for their actions and did not blame their parents. This reflects contrary to Yochelson and Samenow's views that the prison system admonishes prisoners to take personal responsibility for their actions.

"Juvenile Prostitution: A Critical Perspective" by Terrence Sullivan reviews recent, particularly Canadian, legislation which is intended to regulate juvenile prostitution. He describes economic and rational factors in the maintenance of prostitution and the economic self interest of professional groups in defining and serving the "best interests" of young prostitutes. Following the lead of Foucault (1978), he charges that regulation policies ignore the biopolitical economy surrounding juvenile prostitution such as youth unemployment, poor education and juveniles' lack of marketable skills. Highly critical of the commercialization of sex, including juvenile prostitution, in legitimate society, Sullivan attacks government programs as oriented toward punishment rather than protection of juveniles.

Cathie Stivers in "Adolescent Suicide: An Overview" presents a succinct review of the prevalence, demographic variation, causal theories and warning signs of the second leading cause of death among adolescents — suicide. She also poses some suggestions for future research.

Donna C. Hale's "The Impact of Mother's Incarceration on the Family System: Research and Recommendations" explores an interrelationship that has largely been ignored in the field of criminal justice until relatively recently. In order for rehabilitation of the ex-offender into the community to be successful, the returning offender must be rejoining a community where he/she will be supported by a family system or intimate network.

Also exploring this critical relationship as it applies to juvenile offenders is an article entitled: "Juvenile Justice and the Family: A Systems Approach to Family Assessment" by Johnny E. Mc Gaha and David G. Fournier. They present a rationale for, as well as an exploratory study of, a systems approach to family diagnosis in juvenile court settings.

This sampling of provocative articles should whet the appetite of the creative, serious, and ambitious researcher and scholar. The fields of criminology and juvenile delinquency have provided little consensus on causation and control of acts against self, others, and societal institutions. The family and its kin network as an evocateur of deviant behavior or as a caretaking and therapeutic unit capable to assist in the rehabilitation of its rejected members has been one of the most neglected, unrecognized, and tabooed areas of research by 20th century social scientists. On a federal policy and program level there is movement away from large scale systems, organizations, and institutions as central foci of responsibility and control over individuals. The shift is to rely upon smaller units, e.g., families and kin groups, to solve the problems of their dependent and deviant members. This reorientation spotlights families and their extended structures for research probes which search the inner world of small group structure and processes within the context of an ecological framework for explanations of cause, prevention, and treatment of antisocial and criminal behaviors.

REFERENCES

Baumrind, D. (1978). "Parental disciplinary patterns and social competence in children," *Youth and Society*, 9: 239-276.
Bonger, W. A. (1969). *Criminality and economic conditions*, Bloomington, IN: Indiana University Press.
Bordua, D. (1962). "Delinquency and opportunity: Analysis of a theory," *Sociology and Social Research*, 46: 167-175.
Christiansen, H. T. & Gregg, C. F. (1970). "Changing sex norms in America and Scandinavia," *Journal of Marriage and Family*, 32: 616-627.
Christiansen, K. (1968). "Threshold of tolerance in various population groups illustrated by results from a Danish criminological twin study," in A. De Reuck (ed.), *The Mentally Abnormal Offender*, Boston: Little, Brown.
Cloward, R. & Ohlin, L. (1960). *Delinquency and opportunity: A theory of delinquent gangs*, New York: The Free Press.
Cohen, A. (1955). *Delinquent boys*, New York: The Free Press.
Crowe, R. (1974). "An adoption study of antisocial personality," *Archives of general psychiatry*, 31: 785-791.
Currie, E. (1985). *Confronting crime: An American challenge*, New York: Pantheon Books.
Dalgard, O. S. & Kringlen, E. (1975). "A Norwegian twin study of criminality," *British Journal of Criminology*, 16: 213-232.
Datesman, S. K. & Scarpitti, F. (1975). "Female delinquency and broken homes: A re-assessment," *Criminology*, 13, May: 33-55.

Dugdale, R. (1877). *The Jukes: A study in crime, pauperism and heredity*, New York: Putnam.

Durkheim, E. (1951). *Suicide*, New York: The Free Press.

Ellis, L. (1982). "Genetics and criminal behavior," *Criminology*, 20, May, 43-56.

Foucalt, M. (1978). *The history of sexuality*, New York: Vintage Books.

Fox, R. G. (1971). "The XYY offender: A modern myth?" *Journal of Criminal Law, Criminology and Police Science*, 69: 59-73.

Gibbons, D. (1979). *The criminological enterprise: Theories and perspectives*, Englewood Cliffs, NJ: Prentice-Hall.

Glueck, S. & Glueck, E. (1951). *Unraveling juvenile delinquency*, Cambridge, MA: Harvard University Press.

Goddard, H. (1912). *The Kallikak family*, New York: Macmillan.

Goring, C. (1913). *The English convict*, London: His Majesty's Stationery Office.

Hagan, F. E. (1986). *Introduction to criminology: Theories, methods and criminal behavior*, Chicago: Nelson-Hall.

Hagan, F. E. (1985). "Theoretical range in criminological theory," paper presented at the annual academy of criminal justice sciences meetings, Las Vegas, NV, March/April.

Hirschi, T. (1969). *Causes of delinquency*, Berkeley: University of California Press.

Hirschi, T. (1983). "Crime and the family," in J. Q. Wilson (ed.), *Crime and public policy*, San Francisco: ICS Press, 53-68.

Hirschi, T. & Hindelang, M. (1977). "Intelligence and delinquency: A revisionist view," *American Sociological Review*, 42, August: 571-587.

Hutchings, B. & Mednick, S. (1977). "Criminality in adoptees and their adoptive and biological parents: A pilot study," in S. Mednick & K. Christiansen, (eds.), *Biosocial basis in criminal behavior*, New York: Gardner Press: 127-142.

Jacobs, P. et al. (1965). "Aggressive behavior, mental subnormality, and the xyy male," *Nature*, 208, December: 1351-1352.

Lange, J. (1931). *Crime as destiny: A study of criminal twins*, translated by C. Haldane, London: George Allen & Unwin.

Lemert, E. M. (1967). *Human deviance, social problems and social control*, Englewood Cliffs, NJ: Prentice-Hall.

Lincoln, A. J. & Straus, M. A. (1985). *Crime and the family*, Springfield, IL: Charles C. Thomas.

Lombroso, C. (1911). "Introduction" in Gina Lombroso-Ferrero (ed.), *Criminal man according to the classification of Cesare Lombroso*, New York: Putnam.

Matza, D. (1964). *Delinquency and drift*, New York: Wiley.

Matza, D. & Sykes, G. (1961). "Juvenile delinquency and subterranean values," *American Sociological Review*, 26, October: 712-719.

Mednick, S. & Volavka, J. (1980). "Biology and crime," in N. Morris & M.

Tonry (eds.), *Crime and justice: An annual review of research*, volume 1, Chicago: University of Chicago Press: 85-159.

Merton, R. K. (1961). "Social problems and sociological theory," in R. K. Merton & R. M. Nisbet, (eds.), *Social theory and social structure*, New York: Harcourt, Brace and World, 702-723.

Miller, W. B. (1958). "Lower class culture as a generating milieu of gang delinquency," *Journal of Social Issues*, 14: 5-19.

Minuchin, S. et al. (1967). *Families of the slums: An exploration of their structure and treatment*, New York: Basic Books.

Monahan, J. & Splane, S. (1980). "Psychological approaches to criminal behavior," in E. Bittner & S. Messenger (eds.), *Criminology Review Yearbook*, volume 2, San Francisco: Sage, 17-47.

Nye, F. I. (1958). *Family relationships and delinquent behavior*, New York: John Wiley.

Patterson, G. R. (1982). *Coercive family process*, Eugene, OR: Castalia Publishing.

Quinney, R. (1974). *Criminology: Analysis and critique of crime in the United States*, Boston: Little, Brown.

Reckless, W. C. (1961). *The crime problem*, 3rd edition, New York: Appleton-Century-Crofts.

Reckless, W. C., Dinitz, S. & Murray, E. (1956). "Self-concept as an insulator against delinquency," *American Sociological Review*, 21, December: 744-756.

Reid, S. T. (1982). *Crime and criminology*, 3rd edition, New York: Holt, Rinehart and Winston.

Robins, L. N. (1966). *Deviant children grown up: A sociological and psychiatric study of sociopathic personality*, Baltimore: Williams and Wilkins.

Robinson, W. S. (1950). "Ecological correlations and the behavior of individuals," *American Sociological Review*, 15, June: 351-357.

Rosanoff, A. J., Handy, L. M. & Plesset, I. R. (1934). "Criminality and delinquency in twins," *Journal of Criminal Law and Criminology*, 24, May: 923-934.

Sagarin, E. (ed.) (1980). *Taboos in criminology*, Beverly Hills: Sage.

Sarbin, T. R. & Miller, J. (1970). "Demonism revisited: The xyy chromosome anomaly," *Issues in Criminology*, 5, Summer: 195-207.

Satir, V. (1974). *Conjoint family therapy*, Palo Alto, CA: Science and Behavior Books.

Scarpitti, F. R. et al. (1960). "The 'good boy' in a high delinquency area: Four years later," *American Sociological Review*, 25, August: 555-558.

Schrag, C. (1971). *Crime and justice: American style*, Washington, DC: Government Printing Office.

Schuessler, K. F. & Cressey, D. R. (1953). "Personality characteristics of criminals," *American Journal of Sociology*, 55: 166-176.

Schulsinger, F. (1972). "Psychopathy, heredity and environment," *International Journal of Mental Health*, 1, January: 190-206.

Shah, S. A. & L. H. Roth (1974). "Biological and psychophysiological factors in criminality," in D. Glaser (ed.), *Handbook of Criminology*, Chicago: Rand McNally, 101-173.

Stein, M. (1964). *The eclipse of community: An interpretation of American studies*, New York: Harper and Row.

Sutherland, E. H. & Cressey, D. (1974). *Criminology*, 9th edition, Philadelphia: Lippincott.

Tennenbaum, D. (1977). "Research studies of personality and criminality," *Journal of Criminal Justice*, 5, January: 1-19.

Toby, J. (157). "The differential impact of family disorganization," *American Sociological Review*, 22, October, 505-512.

Turk, A. (1969). *Criminality and legal order*, Chicago: Rand McNally.

Van den Berghe, P. (1974). "Bringing beasts back in: Toward a biosocial theory of aggression," *American Sociological Review*, 39 (December): 777-788.

Vold, G. B. (1979). *Theoretical criminology*, with T. J. Bernard, 2nd edition, New York: Oxford University Press.

Vold, G. B. & Bernard, T. J. (1986). *Theoretical criminology*, 3rd edition, New York: Oxford University Press.

Waldo, G. & Dinitz, S. (1967). "Personality attributes of the criminal: An analysis of research studies, 1950-1965," *Journal of Research in Crime and Delinquency*, 4, July: 185-201.

West, D. J. & Farrington, D. P. (1973). *Who becomes delinquent?*, London: Heinemann.

Wilson, J. Q. & Herrnstein, R. (1985). *Crime and human nature*, New York: Simon and Schuster.

Witkin, H. A. et al. (1976). "XYY and criminality," *Science*, 193 (August 13): 547-555.

Yochelson, S. & Samenow, S. (1976). *The criminal personality*, volumes 1 and 2, New York: Jason Aronson.

Family Violence
and Nonfamily Deviance:
Taking Stock of the Literature

Patricia R. Koski

INTRODUCTION

The effect of family relationships on the behavior of children is a classic research issue in the social sciences. With the increasing focus on family violence, social scientists have also become interested in the effects of violent family interactions on children, as well as the related issues of neglect and lack of warmth or caring for children. The assumption underlying these interests is that violent or neglectful families may increase the probability that children will become deviant in some way, and perhaps officially delinquent. Despite increased attention to this issue, many questions are left unanswered.

This paper attempts to answer one important question in this area: is family violence/neglect causally associated with a child's delinquency? While common sense notions and empirical research would indicate a positive correlation, there are enough inconsistencies and methodological defects in the literature to make one pause before accepting an affirmative answer. In this review of recent literature (early 1960s to present), I will examine research findings with the purpose of drawing general conclusions about what is and is not known in this area. While I would argue that there is not yet a clear answer to the question posed above, I would also suggest that

Patricia R. Koski is Assistant Professor, Department of Sociology, The University of Arkansas, Fayetteville, AR 72701.

23

there is much we do know about the effect of family violence on delinquency. However, that knowledge becomes apparent only when the findings from different studies are compared and general patterns emerge from that comparison.[1]

In the following, I will look first at the research on parent-child interactions for each of four types of deviance: aggressive deviance, nonaggressive deviance, measures that combine aggressive and nonaggressive deviance, and adult crime. I will then examine the literature on other family interactions, specifically parent-parent, parent-sibling, and sibling-sibling. Because of the few number of studies done in these areas, I will not consider the four types of deviance separately for each set of interactions. From this review of the literature, I will then offer suggestions as to variables that need to be examined more closely in future research and which should be included in conceptual models predicting causal links between family violence and deviance.

PARENT-CHILD INTERACTIONS

Parental Abuse/Abusive Discipline/Violence

The Child's Aggressive Behavior

In 1964, Becker summarized the then-extant literature as showing a positive relationship between punitive discipline and the child's overt aggression. While his review clearly showed that this relationship is affected by several variables, in general, many studies had repeatedly found an overall link between aggressive discipline and the child's behavior both within and outside of the home.

In the years since 1964, the growing interest in child abuse has extended this research question to include a focus on the effects of less socially acceptable parental behavior, as well as maintaining concern with parental disciplinary techniques. Overwhelmingly, although not without exception (e.g., Bolton, Reich & Gutierres, 1977; Guarino, 1985; Gully, Dengerink, Pepping & Bergstrom, 1981; Reich & Gutierres, 1979), the studies conducted since 1964 have found a positive correlation between parent-child aggression/violence/abuse/physical punishment and aggression on the part of the child. For example, of 14 studies reviewed which dealt specifically with child abuse, abusive discipline, spanking, hitting and yelling, six reported a positive correlation with children's aggression and an additional five reported an association under some more limited conditions (to be discussed shortly). In fact, the link between parent-child aggression and children's aggression is so often found that many researchers either take it for granted (e.g., many of the contributors to Hunner & Walker, 1981) or are willing to accept the link as real despite the serious methodological deficiencies of much of this research (e.g., Smith, Berkman & Fraser, 1980).

Nonetheless, not all research supports this association. Three studies are particularly interesting because of their total lack of support for the parent-child/child aggression relationship (Bolton et al., 1977; Gully et al., 1981; Reich & Gutierres, 1979),[2] while several others report mixed findings (Guarino, 1985; McCord, McCord & Howard, 1961; Straus, 1981; Welsh, 1976). In trying to isolate a variable that might explain these differences, I was struck by the lack of attention specifically paid to gender. In those studies reporting a clear effect of parental aggression on the child's aggressive deviance, most involve samples completely or predominately male. This is not true of the Bolton et al., Gully et al., and Reich and Gutierres studies. Moreover, in those studies reporting mixed findings, the exception to the association often seemed to be the behavior of the females. For example, Straus (1981) found a significant relationship between being hit and the child's nonfamily aggression for boys, but only a slight relationship for girls. Welsh (1976) also reported differences by gender.

In considering gender, one must take into account which parent is abusive. Of those studies involving only single gender subjects, some found differences by the gender of the parent (e.g., McCord et al., 1961; Winder & Rau, 1962). Even though Reich and Gutierres (1979) mention that no sex differences were found in the Bolton et al. study (1977), it seems as least plausible that the sex of the child and of the abusing parent might affect the relationship between parental and childhood aggression. It is not possible to specify yet what these differences might be, but this issue will be addressed again later in this paper.

The Child's Nonaggressive Delinquency

The majority of the research on family violence and deviance/delinquency is concerned only with the child's aggressive behavior. Although there are only a few studies focusing on nonaggressive deviance/delinquency, again those that exist tend to show a positive correlation between the parent's disciplinary/violent behavior and the child's actions, as exemplified by the following studies.

Although failing to find an effect of parental abuse on aggressive deviance, Bolton et al. (1977) and Reich and Gutierres (1979) did find a greater tendency for abused delinquents, compared to non-abused delinquents, to engage in escape crimes (truancy, running away, missing juvenile). Shanok and Lewis (1981) reported more medical hospital visits in a sample of female property offenders than in a nondelinquent control sample, with the clear implication that many of these hospital visits were likely to result from parental abuse. Rhoades and Parker (1981) reported a positive association between child abuse and various forms of nonaggressive delinquency (e.g., drug/alcohol use, running away).

Again, though, a gender effect seems to be a possibility. Straus (1981) found that for males, but not for females, being hit by one's parents was associated with vandalism (but not theft). In a sample of male school children, Winder and Rau (1962) reported withdrawal and depression following punishment by the father, but not the mother. The authors of those studies reviewed which did not report a gender difference often did not indicate the gender composition of their sample or had a majority of one sex in the sample and did not consider the gender of the parent (Reich & Gutierres, 1979; Shanok & Lewis, 1981).

Combined Aggressive and Nonaggressive Delinquency Measures

In some studies, it is not possible to differentiate aggressive deviance from nonaggressive deviance on the part of the child, as the dependent variable includes both types in a delinquency scale. However, on a variety of measures of deviance, the research again supports a positive correlation with parent-child abuse/violence. In a 30-year follow-up to the Cambridge-Somerville study, McCord

(1984) found parental aggression to be associated with juvenile crime. Because McCord's study is longitudinal, it suggests a causal ordering between the parenting (occurring first in time) and the delinquency, although, of course, cause is not therefore established.

Concerning deviant, but not necessarily delinquent behavior, Pfouts, Schopler, and Henley (1981) report similar findings, but again their research suggests that the gender of the abusive parent must also be considered. In their sample, children who were abused only by their mothers were more deviant than those abused only by their fathers or father substitutes. Moreover, those children who were abused by both parents were the most deviant. For children abused only by their fathers, Pfouts et al. report some indication that "abuse from father does not appear to demoralize children to the extent that abuse from mother does but, instead, makes them angry" (p. 96). In fact, the father-only-abused children had the largest percentage (29.4) of the abused sample showing a "balanced relationship style"[3] (p. 97).

Finally, Lewis and Shanok's (1977) report on medical histories of officially delinquent vs. nondelinquent juveniles (crime unspecified) suggests that delinquents made greater use of hospital and emergency room visits than did nondelinquents. Additionally, the medical records of the delinquents indicated greater numbers of injuries in the ages before four and between 14 and 16. Assuming that such injuries could be traced to parent-child violence, the nature of these data suggest a causal ordering. Lewis and Shanok did not find greater perinatal difficulties in the histories of the delinquents; thus it seems plausible to argue that the greater numbers of injuries before age four were due to parental acts. If so, these data suggest that child abuse was prior to, rather than a response to, the delinquency. However, it is also consistent with these data to argue that the increased injuries suffered by the child between ages 14 and 16 reflected the parents' reliance on physically aggressive discipline as a way of controlling the children as they reached puberty. Thus, the theoretical debate as to whether parent-child violence is prior to, or a response to, the child's delinquency may be irrelevant. In fact, parents may rely on their repertoire of disciplinary techniques whenever the child is being punished. If that repertoire includes primarily violent behavior, or violent behavior under the more try- ing instances of child misbehavior, then it is likely to be used as a disciplinary technique in situations both prior to and following de- linquency.

Adult Crime

In addition to deviant behavior on the part of the child following parental aggression, children may grow up to be deviant or criminal adults. Although the research on this topic is particularly sparse, there are some generalizations that can be tentatively offered.

Probably one of the most exciting studies for the examination of parent-child abuse and adult criminality is the longitudinal study done by McCord (1984) and her associates. In 1961, McCord et al. stated that aggressive parents in their sample tended to have aggres- sive (although not necessarily delinquent) boys. After the comple- tion of the 30-year follow-up of these boys, McCord reported in 1984 that aggressive parents in their sample were more likely than others to have children who grew to be adult criminals.

However, there are three other interesting ideas to be drawn from the McCord et al. data that must also be considered before speculat- ing about the effect of parental aggression on the adult crime of these boys/men. First McCord's data indicate that it was still some- what probable that even those children raised by aggressive parents would not become either juvenile or adult officially-labeled crimi- nals (52% were not convicted of juvenile or adult crimes). While recognizing that this misses the point of whether there was a signifi- cant difference between aggressively and nonaggressively disci- plined children, I think it is important to point out that the majority of those children raised by aggressive parents did not grow up to be official criminals.[4]

Second, McCord reports that those married men raised by ag- gressive parents were also more expressive of affection toward their wives than married men in the other two groups. Moreover, men raised in nonaggressive households were least likely to show altru- ism. Is it perhaps possible that being raised by aggressive, or puni- tive but not aggressive parents has positive benefits?

Third, of those men who had been convicted of juvenile crimes, many did not go on to be convicted of adult crimes. Considering men raised in aggressive homes and those raised in punitive but not aggressive homes, respectively, 30% and 15% were convicted of juvenile crimes, but only 18% and 12% were convicted of adult crimes. Only in the group of men raised in nonaggressive homes did the percentages equal each other (6.5% as juveniles, 6.5% as adults). It is interesting, although not easily explainable, to note that the biggest *difference* between those involved in juvenile vs. adult crime was in the category of men raised in aggressive homes. An implication of this is that parent-child abuse may have different consequences for juvenile delinquency than for adult crime.

In fact, other research in this area reports mixed results. Using a sample of college students, Gully et al. (1981) found that parent-child violence was not associated with the students' aggression toward a nonfamily member in the preceding 12 months. Sack and Mason (1980) found that adult sex offenders were more likely to have been abused as children than adults convicted of other felonies.

Clearly, this is a very complex issue, and one that is made even more confusing when it is considered that parental aggression may be only one part of negative parent-child interactions. Of increasing concern is the impact of parental neglect and rejection, the issue to be raised in the next section.

Parental Rejection/Neglect

Although studied less, parental rejection/neglect may be as important as parental violence in producing deviance in the child. In his review of the parent-child discipline research up to the early 1960s, Becker (1964) provided some insights which are still relevant to the topic under consideration here. Becker categorized disciplinary behaviors into love-oriented and power-oriented techniques. Power-oriented techniques (physical punishment, yelling, shouting, threatening) were typically found to be associated with the child's aggressive behavior, as stated earlier. One might assume therefore that love-oriented techniques would not be associated with aggression, but that seems to depend on the type of techniques used and its association with warmth (and thus, also with neglect).

Love-oriented disciplinary techniques may be either positive (e.g., the use of praise or reasoning) or negative (e.g., the withdrawal of love, showing of disappointment, or isolation). In general, the studies in Becker's review found love-oriented techniques to be associated with the child's feelings of guilt for a misdeed, self-responsibility for misbehavior, an increased likelihood of confession, and with nonaggressive behavior. However, this was more true of positive love-oriented techniques than the negative ones. The negative love-oriented techniques were effective primarily when a warm relationship already existed between the parent and child, so that there was love to lose. While this may sound obvious, it has some important implications. First, a hostile or rejecting relationship between the parent and the child might make it impossible for the parent to control the child without physical discipline, thus increasing the likelihood that the parent will resort to physical abuse. Second, Becker found that hostility between the parent and the child affects the extent to which the parent chooses love-oriented or power-oriented techniques. Power-oriented techniques were more likely to be chosen by those parents who were hostile and rejecting of their children. Thus, it may be the case that when the relationship between the parent and child is not warm, disciplinary techniques that do not rely on physical control are less effective and/or the parents are more likely to choose physical discipline. If this is true, then it may be very difficult to separate out the effects of neglect per se and the combined effects of neglect and undercontrol or neglect and physical abuse. This is particularly a problem when the sample studied has come to the attention of the researcher either because of official delinquency or official child abuse/neglect.

On the other hand, when the sample is not officially labeled as neglected, it is difficult to find enough cases of severe neglect to be able to draw any conclusions. Given these twin problems, the best that can be done may be to consider studies related to neglect issues, which use samples from the general population and to compare the conclusions to those studies which used officially labeled samples. That will be the approach in reviewing the following studies.

In a test of differential association, Jensen (1972) set out to evaluate the effects of paternal supervision and support relative to the existence of other factors encouraging delinquency (i.e., the number of delinquent friends, the number of delinquency patterns outside the home, and attitudes about breaking the law). While not strictly a study in neglect, this research does focus on the effect of paternal love and control, relative to other factors conducive to delinquency, and has implications for a consideration of the effects of neglect. Moreover, the sample was drawn from the general (non-black) population.

Jensen found paternal supervision and support to be negatively related to delinquency regardless of the number of delinquent friends the child had and the child's attitudes about breaking the law. Moreover, paternal supervision and support were negatively related to the number of close friends in trouble with the police reported by the child. Finally, the isolated child was more likely to be deviant than the loved child even when there were no strong delinquent inducements outside the home. This study suggests, then, that paternal love and supervision may be of critical importance to male delinquency.

However, Johnstone (1978), in his study of the effect of family integration on delinquency, reached a different conclusion. In this study, Johnstone found that family integration had only a small association with delinquency, with its greatest effect on drug use and status violations. Other more serious offenses were associated with economic deprivation.

Johnstone's study is relevant to a discussion of neglect because his measure of family integration included the closeness of the parent/child relationship, and the number of activities shared by the parent and child. Moreover, like Jensen, this study focused on a sample from the general population.

A significant difference between the Jensen and the Johnstone studies that may help explain the differences in their findings has to do with their definitions of delinquency. Jensen combined several measures of delinquency into a single delinquency score for each

child. Johnstone, however, examined six types of delinquency separately. Johnstone drew different conclusions for the different types
of delinquency, so it is possible that Jensen may also have found his
results to vary if he had examined each type of delinquency separately.

However, both the Jensen and the Johnstone studies are unlikely
to have contained a significant proportion of cases of extreme neglect, given the nature of their samples. Such a caveat is not true of
the study by Pfouts et al. (1981) which focused on families seen by
a Protective Service Unit in North Carolina. While avoiding that
problem, though, the Pfouts et al. study is much smaller and less
representative than the previous two, and it involves a very selective sample determined through official records in a public welfare
unit. Given the Johnstone findings, the single most serious effect of
this selectivity may be the inability to separate out neglect from
economic deprivation.

Nonetheless, the Pfouts et al. study is one of the few directly
focusing on extreme parental neglect. Of the 73 families in the sample, 35.5% were ones in which both the mother and father rejected
the child. Pfouts et al. found that children from these homes were
more deviant (as perceived by the case workers) than children from
homes where there was support and love from at least one parent. In
fact, the most extreme deviance was found in children who were
abused by both parents *and* rejected by both parents. These children
were likely to act out in interactions with siblings, peers, teachers
and parents, to have below average or failing school performance,
to have greater frequencies of criminal and psychological deviance,
and to be the most deviant overall, as reported by the case workers.

Again, then, as suggested by the earlier Becker (1964) review, it
may be important to consider neglect and physical discipline both
separately and together, although it may be very difficult to find
instances of extreme physical abuse which are not accompanied by
parental coldness. One study related to this issue (Deykin, 1972)
did find that the child's behavior differed as a result of different
combinations of neglect and discipline.

Implicit in many of these studies are the assumptions that abused/
neglected children feel more isolated and less loved than other children, and that isolated and less loved children are more likely to

become delinquent. Research generally has not supported the first assumption (e.g., Hancock, 1981), and is mixed with regard to the second.

Several studies have focused on differences between delinquents and nondelinquents with regard to various measures related to closeness to the parents: attitudes toward parents, feelings of being loved or understood, knowledge about the family. In general, these studies have shown that delinquent children are more distant from their parents than nondelinquents (Duncan, 1978; Riege, 1972; Venezia, 1968). Again, there are gender differences. In the Riege study, a majority of both delinquent and nondelinquent females reported feeling more loved by their mothers than their fathers, but more of the nondelinquents felt equally loved by both. Megargee and Golden (1973) found their conclusions to differ by the gender of the parent as well. In their data, Megargee and Golden found that nondelinquents had the most favorable attitudes toward their parents while the psychopathic delinquents had the most negative attitudes. However, the subcultural delinquents (less serious deviance than the psychopathic, but more serious than the nondelinquents) had attitudes toward their mother which were as favorable as the nondelinquents and attitudes toward their father as negative as the psychopathic delinquents.

However, the view that children hold of their parents, and their responses, may be affected by other interactions in the family. In the next section, I will examine the research on interactions between other members of the family, and the impact of those interactions on children.

OTHER FAMILY INTERACTIONS

Parent-Parent Violence/Conflict

This review will focus on the association between parent-parent violence/conflict and nonfamily delinquent/adult crime. Thus, it excludes from consideration the issue of intergenerational transmission of spouse abuse.[5]

The relationship between parent-parent violence and the child's deviance has received only a minimal amount of research attention, despite McCord et al.'s (1961) earlier finding that parent-parent conflict was associated with the aggressive behavior of the nondelinquent males in their sample. In fact, since 1961 there have been only a handful of studies directly focusing on this concern.

One such study of considerable interest because of its sample composition and size is Straus' (1981). Using data from his large (N = 2,143) national sample, Straus found that parental physical conflict was positively associated with delinquency. Another study by Straus (1981) using a smaller sample of high school seniors suggested a relationship between parental conflict and nonfamily assault for boys but not for girls.

In contrast, Gully et al. (1981) found no effect of parent-parent violence on the nonfamily assaultive behavior of college students. The primary difference between the Straus sample and the Gully et al. sample would appear to be (besides relative sizes) the age and class composition of the subjects. Gully et al.'s subjects were somewhat older than Straus'. What differences these two factors might have made can only be speculative, but it is interesting to note that Straus' subjects were still living in the home whereas Gully et al.'s subjects probably were not. If research finds that parent-parent violence is associated with a child's nonfamily deviance, an additional issue must then be considered: does this association maintain itself after the child leaves the home? Again, it is possible that this question might be answered differently for males and females. It is very interesting in this context to note that Gully, Pepping, and Dengerink (1982) found violent females to report observing more parent-parent violence than violent males. If perceptions of violence are important in producing adult aggression, then these differences in perceptions may result in differences in behavior. Additional research is needed in this area.

Other studies reporting on parent-parent violence present a mixed picture. Koski (1984b) found parent-parent but only severe parent-child violence to be more characteristic of juvenile offenders. Pfouts et al. (1981), on the other hand, found victims of child abuse to be more deviant than bystanders to their mother's abuse. Additionally, in the Pfouts et al. study, the bystanders were not as deviant outside the family as they were in their interactions with parents and siblings, although 16% had appeared in juvenile court.

To confuse the picture even more, Riege's (1972) sample of *non-delinquents* reported their parents arguing in front of them more than the delinquents reported. Riege's sample was composed of females, again raising the issues of gender differences.

Parent-Sibling Violence and Sibling-Sibling Violence

Pfouts et al. (1981) report that bystanders to abuse, whether parent-parent or parent-sibling, tend to be less criminal than victims of abuse. In fact, these authors argue that bystanders to parent-sibling abuse often become outwardly "model" children who internalize their stress — showing relatively high rates of depression and anxiety. None of these children had juvenile court records and few had been involved in criminal activity.

Bolton et al. (1977) present data showing the opposite. In their sample, abused children were less likely than their nonabused siblings to have been involved in aggressive crime, whereas the sibling bystanders were less likely than the victims to have been involved in escape crimes (running away, truancy). However, a very large percentage of both the abused children and their siblings had been involved in escape crimes (92.2% and 82.8%). For that matter so were the nonabused delinquent controls and their nonabused, nondelinquent siblings (76.5% and 69.4%, respectively). The Bolton et al. sample of child abuse victims and siblings was much larger (N = 774) than the Pfouts et al. sample (N = 24 children who were bystanders to sibling abuse), so this may explain the differences in their findings.

Using a different type of sample (college students) in which there were probably lower frequencies of extreme parent-child violence, Gully et al. (1981) found parent-sibling abuse not to be associated with the respondents' reports of nonfamily aggression. Rather, these researchers found only self-sibling violence to be able to predict nonfamily aggression. The authors considered parent-parent, parent-sibling, parent-respondent, sibling-respondent, respondent-parent, and respondent-sibling violence in making this conclusion. Moreover, Gully et al. found sibling-self violence to *suppress* self-predicted spousal violence on the part of the respondent. This suggests that the practice a child gets in the home as an aggressor may be important for the likelihood of that aggression being repeated later.

In fact, it may be that the total environment of the home is more critical than the existence of parent-parent, parent-child or sibling abuse alone. Homes in which there is a lack of warmth between parents *and* between parents and children together with some abuse, or in which there is more than one set of abusive interactions may increase the chances of nonfamily deviance. Some work (Rosenbaum & O'Leary, 1981; Straus, 1983a) has suggested that homes in which there is spouse abuse also involve child abuse and sibling abuse. Thus, it may be important to consider as different those homes that have only one set of violent or neglectful interactions and those that have more than one such set. An example of this possibility is the research by Guarino (1985). In general, she found few differences in the delinquency of abused and nonabused juveniles. However, those who had been both victims and witnesses were more likely to commit delinquent acts alone, whereas other delinquents (neither victims or witnesses) were more likely to do so with peers. Guarino suggests that family violence may substitute for peer group influence, but only when the child is *both* a victim and a witness.

DISCUSSION

Earlier in this paper I referred to Becker's (1964) review of the literature on the effect of parental disciplinary techniques on children's behavior. At that time, Becker's review summarized those variables thought to have the most effect on children and reflected the emphasis on parent-child interactions. Since family violence had not yet become a specific topic of interest to social scientists (Pfohl, 1977; Straus, 1983b), Becker's review did not include either an explicit concern with child abuse/neglect nor with other violent family interactions. Nonetheless, Becker's review provides a good starting point for examining what we know about family violence and nonfamily deviance.

Thus, the issue to be considered in this discussion is: given the foundation of research on parental discipline prior to the early

1960s (as summarized by Becker) and the subsequent two decades of research on family violence, what generalizations can be drawn about the relationship between family violence and deviance? Six specific considerations have been suggested by this literature review: the importance of neglect/coldness as well as abuse; the extent to which the seriousness of the abuse/neglect matters; the importance of the total family context of violence and/or warmth; the possibility of different age-related effects; the possible impact of SES; and the importance of gender. Each of these will be discussed in the following.

Generalizations

Neglect/Coldness

Becker (1964) proposed a conceptual model consisting of three continuums describing parental disciplinary behavior. Two of the continuums introduced factors other than physical discipline. While neither Becker's model nor his literature review specifically focused on neglect, both made clear that the effects of physical discipline cannot be seen as independent of factors such as coldness, hostility, permissiveness, and consistency of discipline. For example, in Becker's review, the most delinquent children were those raised in a permissive manner by hostile parents while the most self-destructive children were those raised in a restrictive manner by hostile parents. Thus, hostility seemed to be a negative factor, irrespective of physical abuse, but to have different effects in combination with permissiveness or restrictiveness. To the extent that such factors may be associated with neglect, these findings suggest the importance of considering both abuse and neglect in a consideration of family violence and delinquency.

Since those studies, research focusing more specifically on neglect has generally strengthened the conclusion that neglect and lack of warmth by themselves and in combination with physical abuse are important. However, it remains difficult to separate hostility from abuse, and hostility/neglect from variables such as economic deprivation.

One important idea suggested by this review is that rejection/

abuse by one parent may be mitigated by the love and warmth provided by another.[6] This possibility deserves serious research consideration because of its relevance to policy considerations; that is, should children from violent homes be removed if they are receiving love from one of the parents and if they would then be placed somewhere lacking that love and support? It is possible that this removal from the home may increase the chances of delinquency (Koski, 1984a). Perhaps other action should be taken, as suggested by one child abuse victim: "Why should I have been taken out of the home? . . . My father should have been taken out, not me" (Attorney General's Task Force on Family Violence, 1984, p. 15).

Seriousness of Neglect/Abuse

The studies Becker (1964) reviewed suggested that only extreme cases of hostility and abuse had significantly negative consequences for the child. Again given the difficulty of separating the neglect/abuse from other confounding variables, it is difficult to add much to this conclusion, although Straus' study (1981) shows a greater effect of severe parent-child violence than ordinary violence on male delinquents.

However, the Jensen (1972) study, in particular, does suggest that less extreme forms of neglect may result in (at least) milder forms of delinquency with the potential for more serious deviance. Moreover, depending on how one feels about status violations and juvenile drug offenses, Johnstone's study (1978) may also be interpreted in this way. Perhaps less extreme forms of neglect are more detrimental than the less extreme forms of abuse. This would be an interesting research question.

Total Family Context

Becker (1964) included the idea of parent-parent relations in his model of disciplinary practices. However, it is only in recent years that relations other than those between the parent and child have received scrutiny, and the research remains scarce.

In fact, I would argue that it is this area that should be a major focus of future research. Consistently research has shown a negative effect of witnessed abuse (e.g., Guarino, 1985; Pfouts et al., 1981); these negative effects may be delinquency or internalized aggression. What may be a very important finding is Pfouts et al.'s discovery that 60% of their witnesses to mothers' abuse acted out toward their siblings and 30% acted out toward peers. It is interesting to consider this together with Gully et al.'s data (1981) which showed self-sibling violence to enhance nonfamily aggression and sibling-self violence to suppress predicted self-spouse aggression. If a child *witnesses* abuse of a parent and responds to that by *practicing* abuse on a sibling, this may be the linkage that increases the chances of nonfamily aggression. Moreover, sex-role differences may result in male children taking the role of the aggressor and female children taking the role of victim, thus resulting in an increased likelihood of nonfamily aggression only for males. Perhaps the females would turn to other types of deviance. Hypotheses such as these can only be fully explored if research moves beyond a focus on the relationship between parents and one target child.

Age-Related Effects

Becker (1964) concluded that the age of the child when various forms of discipline occur may be an important variable. Similarly, in the family violence literature reviewed in this paper, there has been a strong hint that violence has different effects depending on the age of children and whether the children are still living in the home. For example, as mentioned earlier, McCord's data (1984) showed fewer adult criminals among those raised by aggressive parents than had been juvenile delinquents.

Because there has been little emphasis on adult crime, it is impossible to draw conclusions about age-related differences. In general, it seems that family violence/neglect has consequences for nonfamily deviant behavior throughout the life cycle, but perhaps stronger effects on the child still living at home. If this is true, there are also policy implications here which, unfortunately, are the opposite of those suggested earlier. That is, leaving children in violent homes may affect their behavior precisely when they are most vulnerable to responding with nonfamily deviance.

Socioeconomic Status

In general, Becker (1964) ignored the subject of SES except for a discussion of the relationship between social class and favored forms of discipline. Since 1964, though, research has implicitly and explicitly shown that the effect of SES on the relationship between family violence and nonfamily deviance cannot be ignored. For example, Johnstone's (1978) finding that family integration was associated only with less severe forms of deviance while economic deprivation was associated with serious delinquency should be kept in mind. In much of the research done to date, serious family violence/ neglect has been coexistent with severe economic deprivation, while samples from the general population involve much milder examples of abuse/neglect. Thus, it is difficult to know the relative importance of SES and severity of abuse/neglect.

Moreover, SES may affect official social control responses to instances of family violence, which in turn affects the likelihood of a child's nonfamily deviance (Gray, 1984). For example, a social control agent may be more likely to remove a poor child from an abusive situation, or more likely to be aware of the abuse than for a child from a wealthier home. If the alternative placement was in a setting lacking the love and control the child may have been receiving from at least one adult, this might increase the chances of the child's delinquency. Another possibility is that social control agents, in responding to a child's delinquency, may be more aware of family violence if the child comes from a poor home and may therefore be less likely to return the child to the home. This would increase the probability that the poor child would be labeled as both abused and delinquent, but would confound the interpretation of causal effects. These possibilities and others related to income variables deserve continued research.

Gender

Consistently throughout his discussion, Becker (1964) found it necessary to qualify generalizations by gender differences. This review, too, has repeatedly emphasized the importance of gender as a variable in the relationship between family violence/neglect and nonfamily deviance. It is unfortunate that more work has not directly addressed this issue.

A consideration of the effects of gender must include, at a minimum, each of the following: (1) the gender of the abused/neglected child or bystander; (2) the gender of the abusive/neglectful or abused parent; (3) the relative effects of same sex parent-child vs. opposite sex parent-child interactions; and (4) the relative effects of parental violence on males vs. females. In many ways our knowledge in this area has not progressed beyond that summarized by Becker. We know that gender matters, but we don't know much more about how or why than we knew in 1964. However, there are some very intriguing recent findings that, when combined, suggest future research agendas.

For example, it would seem that we know very little about which parent causes the most harm when abusive or neglectful. Some find that it is worse for the mother to be abusive or neglectful (e.g., Pfouts et al., 1981), while others find that paternal behavior does have an effect on the child (Jensen, 1972). Interestingly, though, it is often the case that the mother's behavior appears more significant when the samples are composed of both males and females (e.g., Lefkowitz, Walder & Eron, 1963; Pfouts et al., 1981). Alternatively, paternal behavior is found to be important when the sample involves only males (Jensen, 1972). This suggests that mother-daughter, mother-son, father-daughter, father-son interactions are four distinct areas of research and should *not* be considered representative of any general child abuse/neglect processes.

Furthermore, the interactions between the parents may affect each of these four sets of interactions as well as having additional direct effects on the child's behavior. Again, these direct effects may differ by gender. It may be very important in this context that males and females perceive parent-parent aggression differently (Gully et al., 1982). This may be due either to the fact that females are in the home more often to see the violence or that they are more sensitive to the violence, as Gully et al. suggest. Either way, these differences in perceptions of parental interactions may have different effects for males and females. Keep in mind that Gully et al. selected out males and females who had been violent toward a nonfamily member within the last year. We know that females are less likely to be aggressive outside the home than are males. Thus, in a sample of violent males and females, even if they engage in the same behaviors, the females are more deviant than are the males. Thus, not only do these two groups differ in gender, they also differ in the degree of deviance in which they engage. It is tempting to conclude that parental violence affects girls more than boys both in their perceptions and their response to it, but this hypothesis may be overly simplistic. For example one study (Norland, Shover, Thornton & James, 1979) found that family conflict had more of an indirect influence on female than male delinquency (through variables such as reduced identification with parents). This indirect influence was "both greater in total magnitude and wider in scope" (p. 236) than for males. Nonetheless, there was also an important direct effect of family conflict on male property and aggressive crimes.

Whatever the linkage, it would seem critical to keep in mind that males and females often play different roles within the home and it may be these roles, rather than gender per se, that are critical. In fact, rather than focusing on gender as an explanatory variable in itself, research should ask at least: what parent does the abused/neglected child or witness identify with and model? From the perspective of that gender is the child more or less deviant than another child? What role does each parent play in the abuse and how is that consistent with or different from sex-role expectations? What are the consequences of family and nonfamily deviance for males vs. females, both within and outside the home, and how does that affect the child's response to family violence/neglect?

CONCLUSIONS

Before a conclusion can be drawn about the effects of family violence on the child's nonfamily behavior, the questions raised here and earlier in this discussion must be addressed. Of critical importance is the development of conceptual models that would allow research to focus on why and under what conditions abuse does or does not increase the chances of nonfamily deviance. The research to date remains largely descriptive and piecemeal and leads to only one fairly obvious conclusion: unhealthy families tend to produce deviant children, although not always in the ways expected.

However, to say that there is much we do not know about family violence and nonfamily deviance is to make a specious statement. Moreover, it is perhaps misleading. It might be more accurate to say that the descriptive foundation exists to provide direction for the building and testing of conceptual models. It is time now to take stock of what we know and to use that to go beyond description.

NOTES

1. Naturally, in a review of this type of research, methodological issues are of concern. Indeed, it could be argued that family violence and deviance are two of the most difficult sociological concepts to adequately measure. For that reason, any study in this area can be critiqued on methodological grounds. However, I will not specifically address such issues in this paper. My assumption is that when methodological errors differ from research study to study but the same general relationship between independent and dependent variables is found, then one can have increased confidence that perhaps such a relationship really does exist (Freese, 1974). Thus, in this review, I will look for those relationships which are consistently found across studies rather than critiquing a body of research which is all too vulnerable to charges of methodological deficiency.

2. The Bolton et al. (1977) and Reich and Gutierres (1979) papers are actually from the same research project, and the Gully et al. (1981) study might be more properly considered under adult deviance, as its subjects were college students. Because some college students are very close in age to 18, however, the Gully et al. study will be included here as well as later.

3. Of those children who were abused only by their mothers about half lived only with their mothers. The fact that there was no father or father-substitute in these homes might also have had some effect, especially if the child was also rejected as well as abused by the mother.

4. Although they may have had other problems, such as alcoholism.

5. The interested reader is referred especially to Finkelhor, Gelles, Hotaling, and Straus (1983) for a discussion of these concerns.

6. Of interest in this context is whether the child is provided a way to make sense of or justify abuse. For example, Abrams (1981) found no relationship between parental strictness and delinquency but did find an association between perceived unfair discipline and delinquency. Warmth/hostility may be important in the child's perception of the abuse, and this in turn, may affect the possibility of delinquency.

REFERENCES

Abrams, J. R. (1981). Adolescent perceptions of parental discipline and juvenile delinquency. In R. J. Hunner & Y. E. Walker (Eds.), *Exploring the relationship between child abuse and delinquency* (pp. 252-265). Montclair, NJ: Allanheld, Osmun.

Attorney General's Task Force on Family Violence (1984). *Final report*. Washington, DC: U.S. Department of Justice.

Becker, W. C. (1964). Consequences of different kinds of parental discipline. In M. L. Hoffman & L. W. Hoffman (Eds.), *Review of child development research* (Vol. 1, pp. 169-208). New York: Russell Sage.

Bolton, F. G., Reich, J. W. & Gutierres, S. E. (1977). Delinquency patterns in maltreated children and siblings. *Victimology, 2*, 349-357.

Deykin, E. Y. (1972). Life functioning in families of delinquent boys: An assessment model. *Social Service Review, 46*, 90-102.

Duncan, D. F. (1978). Attitudes toward parents and delinquency in suburban adolescent males. *Adolescence, 13*, 365-369.

Finkelhor, D., Gelles, R. J., Hotaling, G. T. & Straus, M. A. (Eds.). (1983). *The dark side of families*. Beverly Hills: Sage.

Freese, L. (1974). *The problem of cumulative knowledge*. Unpublished manuscript. Washington State University, Department of Sociology, Pullman.

Gray, E. (1984, August). *Results of a national research conference on the link between child abuse and juvenile delinquency: The state of the art and recommendations for policy and research*. Paper presented at the Second National Conference for Family Violence Researchers, Durham, NH.

Guarino, S. (1985). *Delinquent youth and family violence* (Publication No. 14, 020-100-74-4-85-CR). Commonwealth of Massachusetts: Department of Youth Services.

Gully, K. J., Dengerink, H. A., Pepping, M. & Bergstrom, D. (1981). Research note: Sibling contribution to violent behavior. *Journal of Marriage and the Family, 43*, 333-337.

Gully, K. J., Pepping, M. & Dengerink, H. A. (1982). Gender differences in third-party reports of violence. *Journal of Marriage and the Family, 44*, 497-498.

Hancock, B. (1981). Offenders' perceptions of childhood abuse and parental motives. *Free Inquiry in Creative Sociology, 9*, 69-71.

Hunner, R. J. & Walker, Y. E. (Eds.). (1981). *Exploring the relationship between child abuse and delinquency*. Montclair, NJ: Allanheld, Osmun.

Jensen, G. F. (1972). Parents, peers and delinquent action: A test of the differential association perspective. *American Journal of Sociology, 78*, 562-575.

Johnstone, J. W. C. (1978). Juvenile delinquency and the family: A contextual interpretation. *Youth & Society, 9*, 299-313.

Koski, P. R. (1984a, August). *The effect of family violence on delinquency: Data, questions and hypotheses*. Paper presented at the Second National Conference for Family Violence Researchers, Durham, NH.

Koski, P. R. (1984b, August). *The role of family violence in explaining juvenile delinquency: An inductive study*. Paper presented at the meeting of the American Sociological Association, San Antonio, TX.

Lefkowitz, M. M., Walder, L. O. & Eron, L. D. (1963). Punishment, identification and aggression. *Merrill Palmer Quarterly of Behavior and Development, 9*, 159-174.

Lewis, D. O. & Shanok, S. S. (1977). Medical histories of delinquent and nondelinquent children: An epidemiological study. *American Journal of Psychiatry, 134*, 1020-1025.

McCord, J. (1984, August). *Parental aggressiveness and physical punishment in long-term perspective*. Paper presented at the Second National Conference for Family Violence Researchers, Durham, NH.

McCord, W., McCord, J. & Howard, A. (1961). Familial correlates of aggression in nondelinquent male children. *Journal of Abnormal and Social Psychology, 62*, 79-93.

Megargee, E. I. & Golden, R. E. (1973). Parental attitudes of psychopathic and subcultural delinquents. *Criminology*, 10, 427-239.

Norland, S., Shover, N., Thornton, W. E. & James, J. (1979). Intrafamily conflict and delinquency. *Pacific Sociological Review, 22*, 223-240.

Pfohl, S. J. (1977). The "discovery" of child abuse. *Social Problems, 24*, 310-323.

Pfouts, J. H., Schopler, J. H. & Henley, H. C., Jr. (1981). Deviant behaviors of child victims and bystanders in violent families. In R. J. Hunner & Y. E. Walker (Eds.), *Exploring the relationship between child abuse and delinquency* (pp. 79-99). Montclair, NJ: Allanheld, Osmun.

Reich, J. W. & Gutierres, S. E. (1979). Escape/aggression incidence in sexually abused juvenile delinquents. *Criminal Justice and Behavior, 6*, 239-243.

Rhoades, P. W. & Parker, S. L. (1981). *The connection between youth problems and violence in the home*. Portland, OR: The Oregon Coalition Against Sexual and Domestic Violence.

Riege, M. G. (1972). Parental affection and juvenile delinquency in girls. *British Journal of Criminology, 12*, 55-73.

Rosenbaum, A. & O'Leary, K. D. (1981). Children: The unintended victims of marital violence. *American Journal of Orthopsychiatry, 51*, 692-699.

Sack, W. H. & Mason, R. (1980). Child abuse and conviction of sexual crimes. *Law and Human Behavior, 4*, 211-215.

Shanok, S. S. & Lewis, D. O. (1981). Medical histories of female delinquents. *Archives of General Psychiatry, 38*, 211-213.

Smith, C. P., Berkman, D. J. & Fraser, W. M. (1980). *A preliminary national assessment of child abuse and neglect and the juvenile justice system: The shadows of distress* (S/N 027-0000-00952-2). Washington, DC: U.S. Government Printing Office.

Straus, M. A. (1981, November). *Family violence and non-family crime and violence*. Paper presented at the meeting of the American Society of Criminology, Washington, DC.

Straus, M. A. (1983a). Ordinary violence, child abuse, and wife-beating: What do they have in common? In D. Finkelhor, R. J. Gelles, G. T. Hotaling & M. A. Straus (Eds.), *The dark side of families* (pp. 213-234). Beverly Hills: Sage.

Straus, M. A. (1983b). Wife-beating. In S. H. Kadish (ed.), *Encyclopedia of crime and justice* (pp. 1629-1634). New York: Free Press.

Venezia, P. S. (1968). Delinquency as a function of intrafamily relationships. *Journal of Research in Crime and Delinquency, 5*, 148-173.

Welsh, R. S. (1976). Severe parental punishment and delinquency: A developmental theory. *Journal of Clinical Child Psychology, 5*(1), 17-21.

Winder, C. L. & Rau, L. (1962). Parental attitudes associated with social deviance in preadolescent boys. *Journal of Abnormal and Social Psychology, 64*, 418-424.

Families Who Kill

Peter C. Kratcoski

INTRODUCTION

Family violence is a documented fact of life in the United States, and the mass media have recently drawn public attention to the physical and sexual abuse of children and to wife battering. Those involved in research on family violence have consistently found that the very factors which make family life appealing, including constant interaction, intimate relationships, emotional bonding, interdependency, and the presence of a hierarchy of power relationships and shared responsibilities, can create tensions which result in violent behavior between family members.

This article focuses on that portion of family violence which has resulted in the death of a family member at the hands of another family member. Although such an occurrence might be considered at first examination to be an unusual event, studies of homicide reveal that it is, in fact, a crime which predominantly involves family members, friends, or close acquaintances. Wolfgang's study of homicides in Philadelphia from 1949 through 1952 found that 65% of all the victims and offenders were family members, close friends, paramours, or homosexual partners, and that 25% of the homicides involved strictly family members (Wolfgang, 1958: 208-213). Pokorny's study of homicides in Houston, Texas, in the years 1958-61, found the percentage of victims killed by a family member or close friend to be virtually the same as that reported by Wolfgang in Philadelphia 10 years earlier (Pokorny, 1965: 479-508). In a study of homicides in Chicago conducted by Voss and

Peter C. Kratcoski is Chair, Department of Criminal Justice Studies, Kent State University, Kent, OH 44242.

Hepburn, 47% of the victims were slain by a family member or a close friend (Voss & Hepburn, 1968: 499-508). A national survey of criminal homicide conducted in 1967 revealed that one-third of the homicides occurred between family members (Curtis, 1974: 50). In Cuyahoga County, Ohio, which includes the city of Cleveland, a study conducted from 1958 to 1974 found that a majority of the homicides involved victims killed by family members, relatives, friends, or acquaintances (Rushforth et al., 1977: 531-538).

Female adults and children appear to be more at risk than male adults with regard to family homicides. In a longitudinal Chicago study (1973-82) it was found that female murder victims were about two and one-half times more likely than male murder victims to be killed by family members. Children were more likely to be killed by family members than were persons from any other age group (Miller, 1983: 23-26).

THEORIES OF FAMILY VIOLENCE

Explanations of violence, as manifested inside the family unit, have included stress theory, systems theory, exchange/social control theory, and social learning theory. Stress theory regards intrafamily violence as the outcome when the natural defenses of persons who are subjected to high levels of stress are inadequate. Intolerable stress levels may be exceeded by pressure from a single trauma or by the gradual accumulation of pressures from many sources.

A study which analyzed the stressful life events experienced by criminal homicide offenders reported that male offenders were more likely than female offenders to have high stress scores on an instrument used by the researchers which examined traumatic losses and other life crises which the offenders had experienced prior to committing the homicides. It was found that white male offenders with high stress scores were more likely to kill family members than nonwhite males with comparable scores. Thirty percent of the white male offenders with high stress scores killed family members, compared to 17% of the nonwhite male offenders with similar scores (Humphrey & Palmer, 1980: 118).

Homicides by females related to stress frequently involve stressful situations between husbands and wives. Instances of battered wives killing their husbands as the catharsis of years of suffering abuse are well documented. Kuhl, in her study of battered women who murder, noted that most women who kill an adult member of their family do so in a defensive rather than an offensive mode. She reported further that the battered woman syndrome has defined such women as "insecure, dependent, nonassertive, self-deprecating individuals" (Kuhl, 1985: 200). The feelings of helplessness in the face of continued and escalating abuse over the years eventually result in a level of stress so high that the homicidal reaction occurs. Warren, in her study of adolescents who battered their parents, also identified accumulated stress as a significant factor in such behavior. She noted that alcohol abuse or other irresponsible activity by parents frequently precipitated such battering, and stated that underdogs in the family, who have suffered repressive treatment, may finally turn to violence as a way of getting attention or having their needs met after all other avenues have been exhausted (Warren, 1979).

A number of researchers have identified stress factors in the family situations of youths involved in threatening to kill or actually killing their parents (Duncan & Duncan, 1971; King, 1975; Sorrels, 1977; Tanay, 1973). They found that the family environments of these homicidal children were characterized by turmoil, physical abuse of children, and constant verbal and physical battles between parents. Hamparian's research on violent delinquents reported them as having poor impulse controls, rage, low self-esteem, lack of empathy with others, and limited frustration tolerance (Hamparian et al., 1978). Kratcoski's study of institutionalized delinquents revealed that 26% of them had experienced physical abuse and that the abused youths were more likely than those who had not suffered abuse to have directed their violence toward members of their immediate families (Kratcoski, 1983).

The finding that the family circle is the location for high levels of stress which is frequently translated into violence underlines the unique nature of the family as a system. Systems theorists note that the family, in a manner similar to a living body, has interrelated parts that support and complement each other's functions. Just as a malfunction of a part of a body affects the entire system and requires adjustment by the other parts if the body is to continue functioning rather than sicken or die, so problems in the functioning of the family as a system can have comparable results. When a family has a set pattern of interaction among members which establishes the limits of the activities of each member and provides mutual satisfaction to the members, it is said to be in a state of homeostasis, and predictable patterns of family interaction are known as homeostatic mechanisms. If disruption of the functioning of the family as a system occurs, these mechanisms are upset, and explosive emotional incidents that result in violence and death are possible extreme results.

Gelles and Straus noted that the family has many patterns of interaction that set it apart from other systems and provide opportunities for violence among group members not available in other settings. These include the many hours each day during which the family members interact, the wide range of activities in which family members are involved together, the demands made by various members of the family who feel they have the right to direct or influence the behavior of other members, the differing ages of the family members, the ascribed roles given to family members by social convention, and the fact that membership in the family is involuntary for many of its members (Gelles & Straus, 1979).

In her study of parricide, Post noted that the onset of adolescence can be an event which upsets the family as a system and affects the entire family in an adverse way. The adolescent's changing physical characteristics, need for privacy, or desire for more freedom may trigger repressive behavior by parents which escalates to violence. Adolescents, aware of their increasing physical strength, may assume the role of protector and try to shield brothers and sisters or a parent from the type of physical or sexual abuse they have experienced at the hands of an adult in the family. Post reported that tensions between the adolescents and parents she studied built up for a period of about six months until the pressures culminated in parricide. She also observed that the families of the homicidal adolescents lacked support from outside friends, relatives, or organizations (Post, 1982: 445-455).

Another key factor in the violence which may characterize the family is the intensity of the emotional involvement and bond between the group's members. Mawson theorized that a great deal of violent behavior within the family can be explained as a tendency or desire to seek the company of a family member at the time when stress is being experienced. This may be true even when the person toward whom the violence is directed is the source of the stress. He used the term "social bonding" to refer to this need, and believed that intense bonding situations could result in such acts as parents' murders of children, sons' and daughters' murders of their parents, or spouse-to-spouse homicides (1981: 12).

Sebastian identified certain social psychological factors as determinants of aggressive behavior in the family setting. He regarded the possibilities of such behavior to be strong because factors that inhibit aggression in the larger society, such as fear of legal consequences, social disapproval, or retaliation, are reduced in the family setting, where the victim may be physically weaker and smaller than the assailant and dependent upon this person. At the same time, factors that instigate violent reactions may be intensified in the family, because of the constant and intense interactions of the members. Expectations set for family members which are not met can trigger violence, but in many instances the family members against whom aggression is directed are singled out because they are helpless to escape from the violence, which is triggered by events outside the family itself. Hel also reported a cost-and-rewards pattern in aggression within the family. Observation of the pain and suffering the offender has inflicted serves as the aggressor's reward, while he or she experiences little fear of costs in terms of legal consequences or social condemnation (Sebastian, 1983).

Blair and Rita Justice, in their study of abusing families, regarded rapid life changes as the key factor in the emergence of family violence. They delineated 43 life events which might occur within a year in a family, some of which were major crises (death of a spouse, divorce, or marital separation) and others which were less devastating. They found that parents who had experienced a large number of life crises within a short period of time were more likely than those who had not to be involved in abusive behavior. However, they also noted that the parents who experienced the most life crises were those who had personality characteristics which brought about many of the crises. For example, the abusive parents tended to be distrusting, impatient individuals with a poor self-image. Their approach to life and their interactions with others precipitated many of the life crises they experienced, such as problems with their spouses, being fired from jobs, default on a mortgage or loan, or trouble with in-laws. Such persons were unable to function effectively within the family system and relieved the frustrations they experienced through violence toward family members (Justice & Justice, 1976: 25-36).

Also related to the existence of violence in the family is the fact that the larger society has, until rather recent times, tolerated violence within the family by both informal mores and laws. The husband had the ascribed position of "head of the household," with the implied duty to assure that his wife and children behaved properly. If methods used to assure such conformity included violence toward wife or children this was allowed, unless the level of violence was evidenced by observable injuries or complaints from other community members. Gelles developed an exchange/social control theory of family violence with reference to this situation. According to this theory, the family is the site where various types of reciprocal, "punishment and costs," relationships are developed. When certain family members are seen by others as not living up to the reciprocal agreement established, anger builds, and conflict and violence may be the result. A husband or father who views his wife and/or children as failing to live up to this agreement may retaliate with aggression.

The exchange/social control theory has particular application to aggression toward family members who are perceived as "different" or nonconforming. These include handicapped, ill, or behavior disordered children and adolescents whom the parent perceives as yielding disappointing results for the investment of time and efforts made in their upbringing. The privacy of family life, the unequal physical strength of family members, and the reluctance of law enforcement or social agencies to pursue family dispute reports all reinforce the possibilities for violence in the family setting. Gelles noted that, although loss of social status may occur if the aggressor is labeled as a wife or child beater, in some subcultures aggressive action to keep family members in line is viewed as evidence of strength or proof that the aggressor is a "real man," (Gelles, 1983). Chimbos, in his study of intraspouse homicide, found that the fatal assault was frequently triggered when the aggressor (male or female) felt threatened or humiliated by the spouse's activities in public, such as flaunting of extra marital affairs or insulting remarks about the spouse. The final assault was frequently the culmination of weeks or months of threats or violence directed toward keeping the spouse in line (Chimbos, 1978: 73).

Social learning theory, as applied to intrafamily homicides, relates to the "generational hypothesis," that is, the belief that early experiences form a child's basic personality that can shape and color all future interactions with other family members. According to this theory, violent behavior is observed or experienced by children within the home, and they come to view it as the appropriate response to problems, internalize this association, and may resort to the ultimate violence, homicidal behavior, when the occasion arises.

Chimbos found that early life experiences of unsatisfactory or frustrating relationships with parents, observation of significant others engaged in physical violence, and participation in such violence as victims resulted in internalization of the idea that violence is an acceptable response to frustration (Chimbos, 1984: 72). Data on 114 violent offenders collected in 1982 and 1983 as part of an URSA Institute project revealed that 30% of the offenders had experienced or viewed wife battering, child abuse, or sexual abuse within their families. Twenty-three percent of the youths were found to have had fathers who engaged in wife battering, 15% had suffered child abuse, and 2% had been sexually victimized in the home (Hartstone & Hansen, 1984: 95).

A study by Lewis et al., of homicidally aggressive young children reported that, in 62% of the households of the homicidal children, the fathers had been physically violent to the children's mothers, and 37% of the fathers of these children had themselves been homicidal. Fifty-five percent of these children had been victims of physical abuse, with 29% abused by their fathers and 25% by their mothers. Nineteen percent of the youths' mothers had been violent toward their husbands (Lewis et al., 1984: 79).

The stress, systems, exchange/social control, and social learning theories of family violence serve as a basis for the inquiry into the nature of the homicides involving family members presented in this article.

THE PRESENT STUDY

The research on families who kill presented in this paper was part of a larger research effort which involved an analysis of more than 2600 cases of non-justifiable homicide. The total project included every case of nonjustifiable homicide recorded in the coroner's office of Cuyahoga County, Ohio, for the years 1970 through 1983.

Cuyahoga County is a highly industrialized area, which is a commercial center. The county includes the city of Cleveland and its suburbs. In 1970, the population of Cleveland was 750,000, and the county's population was 1,721,300. The city's population declined to 563,800 in 1980, a 23% decrease, while the county's population increased 10%, to 1,898,800. In 1980, the population of the county was 82% white, and 18% nonwhite. However, Cleveland, which has 30% of the county's population, had a 56% white population and a 44% nonwhite population in 1980.

Of the victims in the total sample, 31% (831) were whites, and 68% (1797) were nonwhites. Information on race was missing for 1% (5) of the victims. Eighty-one percent of the victims were males, and 19% were females. Seventy-five percent of the homicides were committed with firearms, and 9% by cuts and stabs, with other methods used for the remaining 16%. Forty-two percent of the victims were married, 37% were single, and 14% were divorced. Marital status information was not available for 7% of the victims. In 14% of the homicides, the assailant was a family member. Sixty percent of the family member assailants were spouses, while 40% were other relatives. Acquaintances were the assailants in 40% of the cases, strangers were involved in 14%, and police officers accounted for 1%. In 5% of the cases, more than one assailant was involved. In the remaining cases (26%) the identity of the assailant was not known.

In 45% of the cases, the homicide occurred in the home, in 50% it occurred in public, and in less than 1% it took place in a residential institution (hospital, jail). The location of 4% of the homicides was not available. Forty-five percent of these homicides occurred during or following a quarrel, 11% took place during the commission of a felony crime, less than 1% involved self-defense, and less than 1% happened when the victim resisted arrest. Nine percent occurred in other circumstances, and no information was available on the events surrounding the remaining 33%.

With regard to sex and race, 14% of the victims' assailants were white males, 2% were white females, 44% were nonwhite males, and 10% were nonwhite females. More than one assailant was involved in 5% of the cases, and no information was available on the sex and race of the assailant in 25% of the cases. In less than 1% of the cases, the age of the assailant was estimated to be 5 to 14, in 18% of the homicides the assailant was in the 15 to 24 year old age group, in 27% of the cases the assailant was age 25 to 39, in 14% of the cases the assailant was age 40-59, and in 3% of the cases the assailant was over age 60. In the remaining cases (37%), more than one assailant was involved, or the age of the assailant was not specified.

FINDINGS AND DISCUSSION

This study was exploratory in nature. The data was abstracted from computer data cards located in the Cuyahoga County (Ohio) coroner's office. Information on a limited number of quantifiable variables was collected on each victim, and some data on the assailants was also available. As would be expected when using data of this type, information was missing on various variables in a sizable number of cases. Although the total number of nonjustifiable homicides for the 13 year period exceeded 2600, for this analysis the number of cases in which the assailant was known was less than 1900.

In the analysis, the previous relationship of the assailant with the victim before the nonjustifiable homicide occurred was categorized as family member, acquaintance, or stranger. Cases in which the identity or the relationship of the assailant with the victim was unknown, instances in which the victim was killed by a police officer, and those which involved more than one assailant were excluded from the analysis.

It was found that the characteristics of the victim and the assailant, and the circumstances surrounding the incident when the death occurred, differed significantly when the family-related homicides were compared with those involving acquaintances or strangers.

As shown in Table 1, the sex of the victim was much more likely to be female (37%) in family member homicides than in either acquaintance (15%) or stranger (15%) killings. This finding is consistent with other research on family violence, which indicates that the victims of family violence are most likely to be those members of the family who are the most vulnerable (women and children).

We noted earlier that the larger majority of the homicide victims in the entire sample were blacks. The pattern continued for victims who were killed by family members (72% blacks) and acquaintances (76% blacks), as shown in Table 2. However, the cases of victims killed by strangers revealed a significant shift, with 44% of the victims killed by strangers being white. This finding is consistent with previous research on homicide which suggests that in the largest majority of cases the victim and offender are either related or acquainted and are likely to be of the same race. However, when stranger-to-stranger homicides occur, the racial identities of the victim and assailant are less predictable.

Table 3 reports the marital status of the victim by association with the assailant. As would be expected, a significantly greater proportion of those who were victimized by a family member were married (66%), compared to 39% of those killed by an acquaintance and 46% killed by a stranger. In fact, 60% of those killed by a family member were killed by a spouse.

Table 4 reports the location of the nonjustifiable homicide. It shows that 86% of those killed by a family member were murdered at home, compared to 52% of the acquaintance group and 22% of the stranger group. These findings are also consistent with the findings of previous research, which revealed that for those who are

Table 1

ASSOCIATION BETWEEN VICTIM AND OFFENDER
BY SEX OF VICTIM
(N-1775)

Sex of Victim	----------Type of Association----------						Total
	Family Member		Acquaintance		Stranger		
	N	%	N	%	N	%	
Male	228	62.8%	892	85.1%	311	85.4%	1431
Female	135	37.2%	156	14.9%	53	14.6%	344
Total	363	100.0%	1048	100.0%	364	100.0%	1775

Significant at .001 level, Chi Square test

Table 2

ASSOCIATION BETWEEN VICTIM AND OFFENDER
BY RACE OF VICTIM
(N-1772)

Race of Victim	------Type of Association------						
	Family Member		Acquaintance		Stranger		Total
	N	%	N	%	N	%	
Caucasian	106	29.2%	260	24.9%	160	43.9%	526
Black	257	71.8%	785	76.1%	204	56.1%	1246
Total	363	100.0%	1045	100.0%	364	100.0%	1772

Significant at .001 level, Chi Square test

Table 3

MARITAL STATUS OF VICTIM
BY ASSOCIATION WITH OFFENDER
(N-1755)

Marital Status	---------Type of Association---------						Total
	Family Member		Acquaintance		Stranger		
	N	%	N	%	N	%	
Married	237	66.2%	400	38.4%	162	45.5%	799
Single	87	24.3%	420	40.3%	146	41.0%	655
Divorced	20	5.5%	190	18.3%	30	8.4%	240
Widowed	14	4.0%	31	3.0%	18	5.1%	63
Total	358	100.0%	1041	100.0%	356	100.0%	1755

Significant at .001 level, Chi Square test

Table 4

ASSOCIATION OF VICTIM AND OFFENDER
BY LOCATION OF NON-JUSTIFIABLE HOMICIDE
(N-1753)

Location	----------Type of Association----------						Total
	Family Member		Acquaintance		Stranger		
	N	%	N	%	N	%	
Home	310	86.1%	542	52.2%	78	21.9%	930
Public Place	50	13.9%	495	47.8%	278	79.1%	823
Total	360	100.0%	1037	100.0%	356	100.0%	1753

Significant at .001 level, Chi Square test

high risks for various forms of family violence (wife battery, child abuse) the home is the most dangerous place to be located.

Table 5 reports the mode of killing of the victim in relation to the type of association between the victim and the assailant. As shown in the table, firearms were the predominant mode of killing for all three types of nonjustifiable homicides. However, in family member homicides the killing was more likely to occur as a result of cuts and stabs, or other methods (pushes, falls, asphyxiation, or the use of explosives) than in the other two types. Twenty-seven percent of those killed by family members were murdered by methods other than firearms, compared to 15% of those killed by acquaintances, and 11% of those killed by strangers. This finding is related to the data in Table 6, which summarizes the circumstances of the death, and Table 7, which gives the blood alcohol content of the victim at the time of the death.

Table 6 shows that 71% of the family member cases involved death during or after a quarrel. This was also quite prevalent in the acquaintance cases (66%), but was true in less than one-third of the cases involving killing by strangers. Table 7 shows whether the victim was using alcohol at the time of the incident. Although statistically significant, the differences between the groups are not dramatic when one divides the victims into "no alcohol use" or "alcohol use" as determined at the time the victim was examined by a doctor. Unfortunately, no information is available on the alcohol use of the assailants. The cases in which the victim was a stranger to the assailant exhibited the lowest proportion of cases (35%) in which the victim had used alcohol. The acquaintance category had the highest proportion of cases (51%) in which the victim was under the influence of alcohol.

In regard to the blood alcohol content of the victim, as shown in Table 7, it should be noted that 14.5% of the victims of family members were children, who were of such a young age that it would be unlikely that they would use alcohol. Thus the fact that 41% of those killed by family members had consumed some alcohol takes on added importance. When we consider that 71% of those killed by family members were involved in a quarrel before or at the time

Table 5

ASSOCIATION OF VICTIM AND OFFENDER
BY MODE OF KILLING OF VICTIM
(N-1589)

Mode of Killing	------Type of Association------						
	Family Member		Acquaintance		Stranger		Total
	N	%	N	%	N	%	
Firearms	246	77.1%	809	86.0%	294	89.0%	1349
Cuts and Stabs	56	17.5%	101	10.7%	31	9.5%	188
Other (Pushes, Falls, Asphyxiation, Explosives)	17	9.8%	30	3.1%	5	1.5%	52
Total	319	100.0%	940	100.0%	330	100.0%	1589

Significant at .001 level, Chi Square test

Table 6

ASSOCIATION OF VICTIM AND OFFENDER
BY CIRCUMSTANCES OF DEATH
(N-1876)

Circumstances	Type of Association						Total
	Family Member		Acquaintance		Stranger		
	N	%	N	%	N	%	
During of After A Quarrel	258	71.0%	752	65.5%	111	30.5%	1121
Felony Murder	4	1.0%	24	2.0%	157	43.1%	185
Unknown	52	14.3%	147	12.8%	44	12.0%	243
Other	49	13.7%	226	19.7%	52	14.3%	327
Total	363	100.0%	1149	100.0%	364	100.0%	1876

Significant at .001 level, Chi Square test

Table 7

ASSOCIATION OF VICTIM AND OFFENDER
BY BLOOD ALCOHOL CONTENT OF VICTIM
(N-1792)

Alcohol Amount	Family Member		Acquaintance		Stranger		Total
	N	%	N	%	N	%	
No Alcohol	228	59.7%	515	49.2%	237	65.1%	980
Some Alcohol	64	16.7%	228	21.8%	67	18.4%	359
Legally Drunk	90	23.6%	303	29.0%	60	16.5%	453
Total	382	100.0%	1046	100.0%	364	100.0%	1792

Significant at .001 level, Chi Square test

of the incident, it seems proper to assume that the assailant as well as the victim had consumed some alcohol at the time the incident occurred.

Table 8 gives the sex and race of the assailant by type of association with the victim. Both white females and nonwhite females are significantly more likely to appear as assailants (white 9%; nonwhite 30%) of family members than of acquaintances or strangers. This finding supports the assumptions underlying stress theory. Although women are more vulnerable in family quarrels and arguments and are victimized to a much greater extent than males, the tide may turn in a catharsis situation, where the victimizer on previous occasions becomes the victim.

Table 9 reports the age of the assailant by type of association with the victim. When the age of the assailant was considered in relationship to the three categories of victims, some interesting facts emerged. For all three victim groupings, the age of the majority of their assailants fell in the 15 to 39 age group. It was only when the assailants in the age 40 to 59 and age 60 and over groups were considered that differences in the three groups of victims became pronounced. For example, 7% of the assailants of family members were age 60 or older, compared to 4% of the acquaintance assailants and 3% of the stranger assailants. Again, this finding may be related to the victimization of older family members, who may reverse their roles and violently attack a family member, with death the result.

In summary, although there are a number of gaps in our knowledge about families who kill, one can develop a hypothesis that the patterns and relationships between the assailant and victim are different enough from those found in stranger-to-stranger cases to continue separate investigative lines of research. When developing a profile of the family-related homicide and selecting variables to highlight the contrast of this offense with stranger-to-stranger homicide, the following findings should be considered:

1. While the assailant in all types of homicide cases is typically a young male, in family-related cases there is an emergence of females and older family members in the assailant group.
2. Although the majority of victims in all types of homicides are

male, in family-related cases a sizable proportion of female victims occurs, and more than 14% of the family-related victims were children.

3. In family related homicide cases the majority of victims were married, a factor not true for stranger-to-stranger or acquaintance homicides. The majority of the victims in family homicides were killed by a spouse.
4. The vast majority of those involved in family-related homicides were killed at home, a fact not true for the other categories.
5. While firearms were the predominant mode of death on all types of homicides, family member victims were more likely to be killed by the more personalized methods of stabbing, beating, and strangulation.
6. The more spontaneous nature of family homicides is underlined when one notes the higher proportion of family-related homicides which occurred after or during a quarrel.

CONCLUSIONS

Since this research is grounded in a limited number of variables, it is difficult to speculate on the degree to which the research supports the stress, systems, exchange/social control, and social learning theories cited earlier in this article. The homicide incidents tended to occur in the home, during or after a quarrel, in a spontaneous rather than a planned manner, with the male most frequently the aggressor. This pattern is similar to that identified by researchers who relate family violence to the stress, systems, and exchange/social control theories. It suggests that categories of family members (women, older persons) who are generally thought of as victims can become the assailants. The fact that homicides which occurred in the home were accomplished by stabbing, pushes, falls, or asphyxiation more frequently than by use of firearms seems to support the notion that the activity was spontaneous and therefore stress related. The presence of alcohol in the victim's body in a high proportion of the homicides involving family members and the high proportion of homicides which occurred after quarrels both suggest that the systems, exchange/social control, and social learning theo-

Table 8

SEX AND RACE OF ASSAILANT
BY ASSOCIATION WITH VICTIM
(N-1736)

Sex and Race	Family Member N	Family Member %	Acquaintance N	Acquaintance %	Stranger N	Stranger %	Total
White Male	68	19.0%	199	19.2%	77	22.7%	344
White Female	31	8.6%	22	2.1%	4	1.1%	57
Non-White Male	147	41.0%	669	64.4%	238	70.2%	1054
Non-White Female	107	30.0%	138	13.3%	10	3.0%	255
More Than One Assailant	5	1.4%	11	1.0%	10	3.0%	26
Total	358	100.0%	1039	100.0%	339	100.0%	1736

Significant at .001 level, Chi Square test

67

Table 9

AGE OF ASSAILANT
BY ASSOCIATION WITH VICTIM
(N-1664)

Age Group of Assailant	Family Member N	%	Acquaintance N	%	Stranger N	%	Total
5-14 years old	4	1.1%	12	1.1%	4	1.2%	20
15-24 years old	79	22.6%	260	25.9%	105	33.8%	444
25-39 years old	148	42.3%	410	40.9%	109	35.0%	667
40-59 years old	89	25.4%	238	23.8%	43	13.8%	370
Age 60 and over	25	7.1%	44	4.4%	8	2.6%	77
More than One Assailant	5	1.5%	39	3.9%	42	13.5%	86
Totals	350	100.0%	1003	100.0%	311	100.0%	1664

Significant at .001 level, Chi Square test

ries could apply to these homicides. Since information on the background characteristics of the assailants, such as previous criminal record, socioeconomic class, history of receiving abuse as a child, and mental health problems, was not readily available, one can only speculate on the degree to which a violent response to a frustrating situation was typical behavior for the assailant and related to social learning or stress factors.

We noted earlier that this research was exploratory. A second phase is planned in which the case histories involving family-related homicides will be studied in-depth. A limited number of cases in this group was randomly selected and analyzed. Examination of these cases tended to support both the learning and stress theories. It was found that the assailants who killed family members tended to have previous delinquent and/or criminal records which included violent offenses and to have manifested drug and/or alcohol problems. Evidence that these persons had experienced disruptive family lives was also present in some cases. However, in other cases there was no history of family disorders, no evidence of earlier violent behavior or criminal involvement, and no information about alcohol or drug abuse. In such instances it would seem that the homicide was a crisis situation response to some family occurrence or the catharsis of built-up anger over behavior of the family member-victim.

REFERENCES

Chimbos, Peter D. (1978). *Marital Violence: A Study of Interspouse Homicide*. San Francisco: R & E Research Associates.

Curtis, Lynn A. (1974). *Criminal Violence*. Lexington, MA: Lexington Books.

Duncan, J. & G. Duncan (1971). "Murder in the Family: A Study of Some Homicidal Adolescents," *American Journal of Psychiatry*, 127: 1498-1502.

Gelles, Richard J. (1983). "An Exchange/Social Control Theory," in David Finkelhor et al., *The Dark Side of Families*. Beverly Hills, CA: Sage Publications: 182-192.

Gelles, Richard J. & Murray A. Straus (1979). "Determinants of Violence in the Family: Toward a Theoretical Orientation," in Wesley R. Burr et al., *Contemporary Theories About the Family*. New York: Free Press: 549-581.

Hamparian, Donna (1978). *The Serious Juvenile Offender*. Washington, DC: Office of Juvenile Justice and Delinquency Prevention.

Hartstone, Eliot & Karen V. Hansen (1984). "The Violent Juvenile Offender: An

Empirical Portrait," in Robert A. Mathias (ed.), *Violent Juvenile Offenders*. Newark, NJ: National Council on Crime and Delinquency: 83-116.

Humphrey, John & Stuart Palmer (1980). "Stressful Life Events and Criminal Homicide: Offender-Victim Relationships," *Victimology*, 5: 2-4: 115-120.

Justice, Blair & Rita Justice (1976). *The Abusing Family*. New York: Human Sciences Press.

King, C. (1975). "The Ego and Integration of Violence in Homicidal Youth," *American Journal of Orthopsychiatry*, 45: 134-145.

Kratcoski, Peter C. (1983). "The Relationship of Victimization Through Child Abuse to Aggressive Delinquent Behavior," *Victimology*, 7: 199-203.

Kuhl, Anna F. (1985). "Battered Women Who Murder: Victims or Offenders?" in Imogene L. Moyer (ed.), *The Changing Roles of Women in the Criminal Justice System*. Prospect Heights, IL: Waveland Press: 197-216.

Lewis, Dorothy O., Shelley S. Shanok, Madeline Grant & Eva Ritvo (1984). "Homicidally Aggressive Young Children: Neuropsychiatric and Experiential Correlates," in Robert A. Mathias (ed.), *Violent Juvenile Offenders*. Newark, NJ: National Council on Crime and Delinquency: 71-82.

Mawson, A. R. (1980). "Aggression, Attachment Behavior, and Crimes of Violence," in Travis Hirschi & Michael Gottfredson (eds.), *Understanding Crime*. Beverly Hills, CA: Sage Publications.

Miller, Louise S. (1983). "Women and Murder in Illinois: 1973-1982." Paper presented at the Midwestern Criminal Justice Association annual meeting.

Pokorny, A. (1965). "A Comparison of Homicides in Two Cities," *Journal of Criminal Law, Criminology and Police Science*, 56: 479-87.

Post, Shelley (1982). "Adolescent Parricide in Abusive Families," *Child Welfare*, 61: 7: 445-455.

Sebastian, Richard J. (1983). "Social Psychological Determinants," in David Finkelhor et al., *The Dark Side of Families*. Beverly Hills, CA: Sage Publications: 182-192.

Sorrels, J. M. (1977). "Kids Who Kill," *Crime and Delinquency*, 23: 3: 213-220.

Tanay, E. (1973). "Adolescents Who Kill Parents: Reactive Parricide," *Australian and New Zealand Journal of Psychiatry*, 7: 263-277.

Voss, H. L. & J. R. Hepburn (1968). "Patterns in Criminal Homicide in Chicago," *Journal of Criminal Law, Criminology and Police Science*, 59: 449-508.

Warren, Carol A. (1979). "Parent Batterers: Adolescent Violence and the Family." Paper presented at the annual meeting of the Pacific Sociological Association.

Wolfgang, Marvin E. (1958). *Patterns in Criminal Homicide*. Philadelphia: University of Pennsylvania Press, 1958.

The Criminalization of Forced Marital Intercourse

Robert T. Sigler
Donna Haygood

INTRODUCTION

We are presently observing a change in societal orientation toward sex roles with a major redefinition of the roles of women and the character of societal response and obligations toward women. Criminal justice, along with all other social institutions, is experiencing some degree of confusion as the legal status of acts involving women are redefined by legislative and judicial action. There have been changes in the range of roles available to and exercised by women in crime and in the manner in which the justice system processes women (Adler, 1975). In addition, some acts which have not been included in the list of acts which are processed by the justice system have begun to be defined in criminalistic terms. One set of behaviors which is being redefined is forced sexual intercourse. We have seen a number of changes in the manner in which rape trials are conducted, particularly in procedural rules reducing the admissibility of evidence about the victim. The defenses available to the accused are becoming restricted, with factors such as prior relationships becoming less effective. In particular there has been pressure for restriction of the use of marital status as a defense in rape. It is the purpose of this paper to explore the present status of forced marital intercourse, public perception of forced marital intercourse, and public preferences for strategies to control the use of

Robert T. Sigler is Associate Professor, Department of Criminal Justice, The University of Alabama, 436 Farrah Hall, Box 6365, University, AL 35486. Donna Haygood is a graduate student at the College of William and Mary.

force to gain sexual access in relatively intimate relationships between men and women.

Forced marital intercourse lies at the intersection of two of the most salient issues for criminal justice as it relates to women's rights and the new feminism: the manner in which the justice system responds to rape (Brownmiller, 1975; Clark & Lewis, 1977; Cornell & Wilson, 1974) and spouse abuse (Davidson, 1978; Fleming, 1979; Langley & Levy, 1978; Pagelow, 1981; Walker, 1979). Forced marital intercourse became salient in 1978 in the State v. Rideout case (Or. Cir. Ct., Freeman, 1981) in Oregon in which the marital immunity defense was challenged by the state.

Historically women have been defined as subordinate to men. Men were expected to discipline their wives and had the right to use reasonable physical force including such acts as "a broken nose for an unwashed dish or a black eye for a cross word" (DoBash & DoBash, 1979, p. 61). In this context it can be seen that the use of force to compel a woman to fulfill her duties as a wife would be seen as a reasonable use of disciplinary force. Early involvement of the justice system in the control of forced sexual intercourse was based on the property rights of the male on whom the female was dependent. That is, the crime of rape was a crime against men, because women were owned by men and were not independent human beings (Brownmiller, 1975). Under Anglo-Saxon law the penalty for rape was a fine which was paid to the husband or father for the loss of value to his property caused by the rape (Clark & Lewis, 1977). As women have gained independence and status in the eyes of the law this frame of reference for judging acts against women has and is gradually evolving both within the justice system and in the eyes of the public. Rape as traditionally defined is being replaced by or supplemented by attention to a broader range of acts.

Forced sexual intercourse includes behaviors which range from the use of force by a stranger to gain sexual access in a sudden unanticipated encounter to the use of force by a man to gain access to his wife in their home. The tendency to categorize forced marital intercourse as rape creates more confusion in an already confusing array of mitigating circumstances considered relevant in law to the determination of rape and in the eyes of the public in assigning blame to the woman. The woman who is the victim of forced sexual intercourse is held responsible if she implies consent, does not resist, behaves in a manner which invites attack, or has given contractual consent in marriage or by participating in a long-term relationship such as living with her attacker. Barnett and Field (1977) found that 38% of the female college students and 59% of the male college students in their sample believed that women provoke rape by their appearance or behavior. The issue of legal control of forced marital intercourse thus is complicated by arguments which address culpability and victim participation in rape.

Still, there appears to be growing public sentiment for control of forced marital intercourse. It has been proposed that the predominance of the patriarchal system and the widespread acceptance of a traditional ideology which supports dependency of females on males are the principle reasons for the enduring immunity from prosecution for husbands who force their wives to submit to sexual activity. At present 10 states give specific immunity to the husband, five states recognize immunity under common law rulings, 30 states provide partial immunity, and four states have laws which specify no immunity for husbands (National Center on Family Law, 1980). In many cases the no immunity or only partial immunity status has been effected by recent legislative or public support for the criminalization of forced marital intercourse. This is reinforced by a study by Teske, Williams, and Dull (1980) which found that two-thirds of the studied sample were opposed to a law which would permit a wife to charge her husband with rape.

The rationale behind public opinion regarding legislation addressing this issue appears to be based on two beliefs: the degree of wrongness inherent in the act itself and the viability of a criminal sanction for dealing with the behavior (Jeffords, 1981). The concern itself can be seen as a result of the reduction in the predominance of the patriarchal system and the acceptance of the traditional ideology which supports subordinate and dependent roles for women which has emerged from the most recent surge of interest in women's liberation. In essence, the ideology which gives a degree of normative acceptance to rape and to spouse abuse which links this cultures sex roles of male dominance and female submissiveness with these acts (Brownmiller, 1975; Clark & Lewis, 1977) has been weakened as women gained access to the workplace, freedom from legal male dominance in marriage, and greater personal freedom in the 1960s and 1970s. In the turmoil over the equal rights for women movement, public perceptions of women created a condition in which the public is willing to accept challenges to establish cultural principles as evidenced by the recent furor over the Rideout case.

With perceived public support of the criminalization of forced marital intercourse the impact of groups and individuals who promote legislation to restrict spousal immunity with state legislation has increased. This pressure to promulgate new laws should be evaluated in the context of the purpose of the law and in the arguments which support and oppose spousal immunity.

Secondly, the purpose of criminal law is to prevent certain undesirable conduct and thus protect various interests of society (LaFave & Scott, 1972, p.21). By this characterization forced marital intercourse should be defined as undesirable behavior which threatens the interest of society if legislation is required. The law to some extent reflects changing value systems but moves slowly so that enduring changes in values evolve into law while fleeting value shifts do not (Tappen, 1947). Of course most value shifts are not reflected in law. Our system of laws is only invoked when some value shifts are resisted and require the power of the law for enforcement (Travis, 1973). It is possible for active groups to press for formalization of their special interests leading to laws which may serve to protect the personal values of the interest group rather than the interests of society (LaFave & Scott, 1972). Feminists note that legislatures are dominated by men who tend to represent the special interests of men to the detriment of women (Brownmiller, 1975; Cornell & Wilson, 1974; Russell, 1975). The present trends are seen as necessary to develop a fair and balanced system to protect women's rights.

The issue of spousal immunity has been debated in the literature. The degree of wrongness of the act and the effectiveness of legislation in accomplishing control have been challenged. Within the framework of traditional ideology, the husband has a property or contractual right to sexual access. In State v. Smith (372 A.2d 386,

1977) the court argued that if a wife can exercise a legal right to separate from the husband and to terminate the marriage contract, then she can also revoke a term of that contract, such as consent to intercourse. It should be noted that states with partial immunity withdraw that immunity at some point in the separation process leading to divorce.

Women are harmed by forced marital intercourse. In addition to physical harm, the women who experience forced marital intercourse can be harmed emotionally. Russell (1975) asserts that marital rape is one of the most traumatic experiences a woman can have. Forty percent of the victims he interviewed who had not suffered physical damage reported that they were extremely upset by the incident. It can also be argued, however, that any close relationship produces a variety of traumatic confrontations which are a part of a marital relationship and which are not subject to societal intervention. That is, society does not have a legitimate interest in intervention or control of acts which occur within a marital context. In addition, a complaint or prosecution for forced marital intercourse would reduce the chances of reconciliation (Horton, 1966). The appropriate remedy becomes separation or divorce. Divorce is not feasible in some cases for religious, social, and economic reasons (Klatt, 1980) and is difficult to obtain in other cases (Glasgow, 1980).

The relationship between law and control is unwritten. In our present system there is a general problem of over legislation and over criminalization. It is also possible that a law prohibiting forced marital intercourse would not be enforced. Fleming (1979) and Woods (1978) note that assault laws in cases involving spouses are not presently enforced. Add to that the difficulties involved in securing a rape conviction when a close personal relationship is an element and it appears probable that forced marital intercourse laws would not be enforceable. The problem of proof would be a major liability for any successful action (Glasgow, 1980; Schultz, 1978). It is possible that the presence of such law would lead to abuse through attempts at spouse control by the filing of false complaints (State v. Smith, 372 A.2d, 1977).

With legislatures reviewing spousal immunity there is a need to expand our understanding of the phenomenon of forced marital intercourse and to assess contemporary public orientation toward forced marital intercourse and its control. Research in this area has been limited but indicates some shift in public perception regarding forced marital intercourse. The study reviewed here represents an attempt to expand our knowledge in this area.

METHODOLOGY

This study was designed to be a descriptive, exploratory survey project. A questionnaire was administered to a randomly drawn sample of adults in Tuscaloosa, Alabama. Tuscaloosa with a population of about 100,000, has two universities, a junior college, three state mental health institutions, and a light and medium industry base.

The sample of adult subjects was drawn from a population of all residential units in the city of Tuscaloosa. Multistage cluster sampling was used with grids, blocks, and residences as the units. A random sample of blocks was taken from each grid. A random sample of houses was taken from each block. Questionnaires were distributed to all residents over 18 years of age in the sampled houses. The use of residences as the basic unit was designed to produce a sample of permanent residents with minimal student representation. Comparison of the sample statistics with census statistics indicated that the sample was biased in that more females were selected. The sample was younger, tended to have more marrieds, more retired subjects, and a higher income than the census sample. This is attributed to the deliberate underselection of students and institutionalized adults in the Tuscaloosa area.

The instrument was a 63-item questionnaire designed to measure public attitudes toward forced marital intercourse, orientation towards traditional sex roles, and a set of demographic variables. Subjects were notified of their selection by postcard. The questionnaires were delivered to the homes of the subjects and were collected at the homes about four days later. Three hundred questionnaires were delivered to 177 homes. One hundred and eighty-one questionnaires were returned by the subjects. Of these, 15 were incomplete and were dropped from the study leaving a sample of 166.

FINDINGS

Data were collected on a number of variables which are potentially related to the subject's willingness to endorse legislation designed to control forced marital intercourse and the type of penalty the subjects assigned to types of forced sexual intercourse. Preliminary analysis identified a number of bivariate relationships among the variables of interest. To clarify the relationship between the independent variables and the dependent variables two discriminant analyses were performed. While discriminant analysis has been recognized as a powerful statistical tool in applied settings, there has been little use of this statistical procedure in nonapplied research. Discriminant analysis permits the evaluation of the combined influence of a number of interval independent variables on an ordinal or nominal dependent variable. Endorsement of legislative action is a nominal variable and the measure of penalty assigned to forced marital intercourse as compared to the penalty assigned to rape is an ordinal variable. Thus, discriminant analysis is the appropriate procedure for exploratory analysis of this data set. Nominal and ordinal independent variables were expressed in dichotomized 1,0 format for inclusion in the analysis.

In addition to demographic variables and a number of direct measures of subject's beliefs, three Guttman type scales were designed to measure belief in traditional roles for women, extent to which women should be able to refuse sexual access, and the extent to which forced marital intercourse is seen as wrong. Traditional roles for women demonstrated a coefficient of reproducibility of .9470 after one item was dropped from the scale. Refusal of sexual access demonstrated a coefficient of reproducibility of .9711. Perception of forced marital intercourse as wrong demonstrated a coefficient of reproducibility of .9849; however, the items were negatively associated, so this scale was dropped from further analysis.

The items in the traditional roles for women scale are presented in Table 1. While the scale adequately discriminates between subjects, the rate of endorsement of traditional roles is relatively high with over three-fourths of the subjects placing women in the home and out of leadership positions. The items for refusal of sexual access are presented in Table 2. These subjects also demonstrate a

Table 1

Frequency of Positive Endorsement of
Traditional Women's Sex Role Items

Item	N	%
Women are not as legitimate as men in political office	146	88
Males should be leaders in mixed groups	131	78.9
Woman's place is in the home	129	77.7
The husband should make decisions	90	54.2
Women should obey their husbands	74	44.6

Table 2

Frequency of Endorsement of Reasons for
Refusal of Sexual Access by Wives

Reason	N	%
Sick	165	99.4
Tired	153	92.2
Mad	139	83.7
Any time	131	78.9
Manipulation	129	77.7

high level of endorsement with over three-fourths of the subjects endorsing all items.

These subjects were willing to endorse a felony penalty for most forms of forced sexual intercourse. Table 3 presents the endorsement of a felony penalty by degree of association when physical injury occurs and when physical injury does not occur. In both cases as the degree of association decreases, the percentages of subjects endorsing a felony penalty decreases with the exception of the victim who is picked up but not physically injured.

Table 4 presents the subjects' placement of the appropriate penalty for forced marital intercourse in relation to the penalty for rape with two nonrape related categories designed to establish the lower range of the scale. The second dependent variable was formed from two items, endorsement of legislation criminalizing forced marital intercourse at the felony level and endorsement of legislation criminalizing forced marital intercourse at the misdemeanor level. Fifty-five (33.1%) subjects endorsed felony legislation and 80 subjects (45.2%) endorsed misdemeanor legislation. The new scale groups all subjects who endorsed felony legislation (55 subjects), all subjects who endorsed misdemeanor legislation but not felony

Table 3

Frequency of Endorsement of a Felony Penalty
for Forced Sexual Intercourse with and without Injury
for Differing Degrees of Association between Actors

Degree of Association	With Injury		Without Injury	
	N	%	N	%
Stranger	162	97.6	157	94.6
Pickup	155	93.4	114	68.7
Dating	147	88.6	121	72.9
Divorce	141	84.9	120	72.3
Separated	125	75.3	97	58.4
Married	91	54.8	53	31.9

Table 4

Frequency of Endorsement of Penalties for
Forced Marital Intercourse Relative to Rape

Item	N	%	Cumulative %
no penalty	23	13.9	13.9
grounds for divorce	54	32.5	46.4
less than rape	46	27.7	74.1
equal to rape	29	17.5	91.6
greater than rape	14	8.4	100.0
	166	100	

legislation (39 subjects), and subjects who endorsed neither felony nor misdemeanor legislation (72 subjects).

Tables 5a, 5b, and 5c present the results of a discriminant analysis with endorsement of legislation as the dependent variable. The first function tends to differentiate the groups endorsing a misdemeanor penalty from the other two groups. Both the group which supports felony legislation and the group which supports misdemeanor legislation appear to believe that people would see forced marital intercourse as wrong if it were against the law, endorse a felony penalty for rape when there is force but no physical injury, and tend to believe that a law controlling forced marital intercourse would have a preventive effect. These two groups differ on a number of variables including race, sex, and church attendance. Males, blacks, and those with high church attendance tend to favor felony legislation while females and whites tend to favor misdemeanor legislation. Those who believe that a wife should control sexual access, who see rape as an assaultive act, who see forced marital intercourse as a family issue, but who do not see present laws controlling rape as effective favor misdemeanor legislation. Those who

Table 5a

Canonical Discrimination Functions for Predicting Endorsement of Felony or Misdemeanor Legislation to Control Forced Marital Intercourse

Function	Eigen Value	Percent of Variance in Eigen Value	Canonical Correlation	After Function	Chi Squared	D.F.	Significance
0	.39314	70.20	.5312212	0	76.776	22	< .001
1	.16692	29.80	.3782087	1	24.390	10	≤ .001

Table 5b

Standardized Canonical Discriminant Function Coefficients

Variable	Function 1	Function 2
Sex: Male	.40754	-.24257
Race: Black	.04766	-.71442
Church attendance	.61793	-.02050
FMI is a family matter	-.18110	.24682
People would see FMI as wrong if it were against the law	.47205	.35442
Penalty for rape when force is used without physical injury	.42120	.39351
Rape is an assaultive act	-.34791	.54407
Laws are effective in preventing rape	.47055	.31340
A law controlling FMI would be enforced	.29869	.09985
A law would be effective in preventing FMI	.16837	.35577
Right of wife to refuse sexual access	.05559	.41583

Table 5c

Canonical Discriminant Functions Evaluated at Group Means (Group Centroids)

Type of Law Enforced	Function 1	Function 2	N
No penalty	-.44179	-.36201	72
Misdemeanor	-.42913	.67494	39
Felony	.88263	-.00457	55

see rape as a sexual act, who believe that laws controlling rape are effective, and who believe that a law controlling forced marital intercourse would be enforced endorse felony legislation.

The second discriminant analysis examined the relationship between disposition of forced marital intercourse offenders and the variables of interest to this study. The results of this analysis are presented in Tables 6a, 6b, and 6c. Function 1 tends to differentiate between groups endorsing a criminal penalty and groups endorsing no penalty or a civil remedy. White subjects, male subjects, and lower income subjects tend to endorse noncriminal dispositions. This position also appears to be associated with the perceptions of forced marital intercourse as a family issue, the belief that a law controlling forced marital intercourse would be enforced, and endorsement of traditional roles for women. The association with penalties for rape is unclear with subjects in the noncriminal groups appearing to favor a felony penalty for rape in which physical injury occurred and when threat of force was used but not when force was actually used without physical injury.

Function 2 appears to differentiate between the no penalty groups and the basis for divorce group. In addition to race, the no penalty group is characterized by a belief that forced marital intercourse would not be seen as wrong if it were against the law, the endorsement of a felony penalty for rape in which physical injury occurs, a belief that rape laws are ineffective, and a belief that a law controlling forced marital intercourse would not be effective. Function 3 appears to differentiate between the group endorsing criminal penalties greater than or equal to those for rape and the group endorsing a criminal penalty less than rape. The group endorsing the lesser criminal penalty tended to be older, perceived rape as an assaultive act, and tended to endorse penalties less than felony for rape when physical injury did not occur.

DISCUSSION

The exploratory study has examined public perceptions about the appropriate disposition of forced marital intercourse. This sample appears to support the criminalization of forced marital intercourse

Table 6a

Canonical Discriminant Functions for Penalty for Forced Marital Intercourse
in Relation to the Penalty for Rape

Function	Value	Percent of Variance in Eigen Value	Canonical Correlation	After Function	Wilks Lambda	Chi Squared	D.F.	Significance
0	.88654	69.59	.6855	0	.3749	153.05	42	≤ .001
1	.29868	23.45	.4769	1	.7073	54.03	26	≤ .001
2	.08873	6.96	.2855	2	.9185	13.26	12	.35
3				3				

Table 6b

Standardized Canonical Discriminant Function Coefficients

Variables	Function 1	Function 2	Function 3
Sex: Male	.39235	-.19255	-.13109
Age	.17228	.14284	.46451
Race: Black	-.38910	.34596	-.30500
Grade	-.18906	-.26157	.25049
Income	-.33961	-.10981	.28708
Family issue	.32841	.05819	.20221
FMI would be seen as wrong if against the law	-.24111	-.51556	.20517
Felony penalty for rape when:			
Physical injury occurs	.34229	.56784	.11416
Force but no injury	-.55188	-.15493	-.37918
Threat but no force	.43985	.07430	-.30297
Rape is an assaultive act	-.05864	.37851	.80580
Rape laws are effective	.15410	.69182	-.01384
A FMI law would be enforced	-.39187	-.39228	-.22954
Traditional roles for women	.50901	-.26771	-.09857

Table 6c

Canonical Discriminant Functions
Evaluated at Group Means
(Group Centroids)

Group	Function 1	Function 2	Function 3
No penalty	1.50630	1.01781	-.05949
Grounds for divorce	.73603	-.64620	.03643
Criminal less than rape	-.83278	.20355	.37969
Criminal equal to or greater than rape	-.83913	.04935	-.42010

with about 57% of the subjects endorsing either the passage of a statute making forced marital intercourse a felony or the passage of a statute making it a misdemeanor offense. About one-fourth of this sample classified forced marital intercourse as at least as serious as rape.

Forced marital intercourse has been characterized in this study as one category of forced sexual intercourse. Forced sexual intercourse has been compared with degree of association. As forced sexual intercourse moves from attack by a stranger to forced intercourse by a husband, the extent to which subject endorsed a felony penalty decreased. Thus, degree of association can be seen as a mediating factor in forced sexual intercourse with possible attribution of increasing responsibility to the victim or with possible reduction in the extent to which the behavior is perceived as wrong as the degree of personal involvement increases. When physical injury is added, the pattern remains essentially the same with the degree of endorsement of a felony lower in each case when physical injury does not occur. It is noted that this sample appeared to have less sympathy for a woman who was raped without injury after being picked up than with the date rape or the divorced woman who is forced by her ex-husband.

The two discriminant analyses which were used to explore the relationships between the set of demographic and attitudinal variables and endorsement of legislation and types of penalty revealed a number of factors. There does appear to be a relationship between attitudes about the effectiveness of the law and both the endorsement of criminalization and the degree of sanction endorsed. Those who believe that the existing laws are effective and that proposed laws will be effective endorse legislation with stronger penalties for forced marital intercourse and endorse higher penalties. When belief in effectiveness of laws is absent, subjects endorse lower levels of sanction. A similar pattern is seen when the ability of a new law to change attitudes about forced marital intercourse is assessed. Traditional views of women appear to be associated with setting high penalties but not with endorsement of legislation while the right of a wife to control sexual access is associated with endorsement of legislation but not severity of sanction.

SUMMARY

This exploratory study of public perceptions of forced sexual intercourse has indicated that there is some support for the criminalization of this behavior. Attitudes about the traditional role of women, the effectiveness of the law, the perceptions of rape as an assaultive act, and the right of wives to control sexual access appear to be associated with endorsement of legislation and the degree of sanction endorsed. Further research which will clarify the specific nature of the set of attitudes which influence perceptions of forced marital intercourse is warranted.

REFERENCES

Adler, F. (1975). *Sisters in crime*, New York: McGraw-Hill Book Company.

Barnett, N.J. & Field, H.S. (1977). Sex differences in university students' attitudes toward rape. *Journal of College Student Personnel*, 18(2), 93-96.

Brownmiller, S. (1975). *Against our will: Men, women, and rape*, New York: Simon and Schuster.

Clark, L.M. & Lewis, D.J. (1977). *Rape: The price of coercive sexuality*, Toronto: Women's Education Press.

Cornell, N. & Wilson, C. (1974). *Rape: The first sourcebook for women*, New York: The New American Library.

Davidson, T. (1978). *Conjugal crime*, New York: Ballantine Books.

DoBash, R.E. & DoBash, R. (1979). *Violence against wives: A case against patriarchy*, New York: The Free Press.

Fleming, J.B. (1979). *Stop wife abuse*, Garden City, NY: Anchor Press/Doubleday.

Glasgow, J.M. (1980). The marital rape exemption: Legal sanction of spouse abuse. *Journal of Family Law*, 18 (April), 585-586.

Jeffords, C.R. (1981). Demographic variations in attitudes toward marital rape immunity. Survey Research Program, Texas Criminal Justice Center, Sam Houston State University.

Jeffords, C.R. (1982). Public attitudes toward criminal sanctions against forced marital intercourse. Paper presented at the Academy of Criminal Justice Sciences Conferences.

Horton, J. (1966). Order and conflict theories of social problems as competing ideologies. *American Journal of Sociology*, 71(6), 701-713.

Kercher, G.A., Jeffords, C.R. & Dull, R.T. (1981). Legislative proposals about crime and criminal justice: Texas Crime Poll, 1980. Survey Research Program, Texas Criminal Justice Center, Sam Houston State University.

Klatt, M.R. (1980). Rape in marriage: The law in Texas and the need for reform. *Baylor Law Review*, 32 (Winter), 109-121.

LaFave, W.R. & Scott, A.W. (1972). *Handbook on criminal law*, St. Paul, MN: West Publishing Co.

Langley, R. & Levy, R.C. (1978). *Wifebeating: The silent crisis*, New York: Pocket Books.

National Center on Women and Family Law (1980). Untitled mimeograph, New York.

Pagelow, M.D. (1981). *Women and crime*. New York: Macmillan Publishing Co., Inc.

Russel, D.E. (1975). *The politics of rape: The victim's perspective*, New York: Stein and Day.

Schultz, S.L. (1978). The marital exception to rape: Past, present and future. *Detroit College of Law Review* (Summer), 261-276.

Tappen, P.W. (1947). Who is the criminal. *American Sociological Review*, 12(1), 96-102.

Tavis, C. (1973). Who likes women's liberation and why: The case of the unliberated liberals. *Journal of Social Issues*, 29(4), 175-198.

Teske, R.H. Jr., Williams, F.P. & Dull, R.T. (1980). Texas Crime Poll Spring 1980 Survey. Criminal Justice Research Center, Sam Houston State University.

Walker, L.E. (1979). *The battered woman*, New York: Harper & Row.

Woods, L. (1978). Litigation on behalf of battered women. *Women's Rights to Law Reporter*, 5(1), 7-15.

CASES

State v. Rideout, Or. Cir. Ct., cited in Freeman (1981).

State v. Smith, 372 A.2d 386 (1977).

Immer v. Risks, 267 A.2d 481 (1970).

The Victim-Offender Relationship: A Determinant Factor in Police Domestic Dispute Dispositions

Daniel J. Bell

INTRODUCTION

The study of the family as a social group suggests that it is pre-eminent in several types of violence, i.e., slaps, torture, rape, and murder (Straus, 1974). Also, the study of contemporary American society identifies the family as the primary social setting for aggression and violence (Straus, 1977). However, historically, there has been some difficulty in estimating the extent of domestic violence. Even so, Gaquin (1978) reported that 150,000 individuals are assaulted each year by a spouse or ex-spouse and more than half of these incidents (55%) are reported to the police.

Recent literature indicates that domestic violence is not an isolated event that occurs outside the context of everyday family life. Straus (1974) reported that couples who verbally express their dissatisfactions are more likely to be physically violent. Also, Straus (1979c) noted that 16 per 100 spouses are violent in one year and 6.1 per 600 of these are severe and 63.5 per 100 parents are violent toward their children and 14.2 per 100 of these are severe. In contrast, children are violent toward their parents 18 per 100 and 9.5 per 100 of these are severe. In addition, children are violent with each other 79.9 per 100 in one year and 53.2 per 100 of these are

Daniel J. Bell is Associate Professor of Criminal Justice, Southwest Texas State University, San Marcos, TX 78666.

87

severe. Additional findings include: (1) mothers abuse 17.7 per 100 children, (2) fathers abuse 10.1 per 100 children, however, women are home more often than men and have more opportunity to be abusive with their children, and (3) male children are punished twice as frequently as females.

O'Brien's (1971) study of divorced individuals reported that violence was the primary reason for divorce in 15% of the cases. O'Brien's study consisted of middle class couples who had been married 2.7 to 20.6 years. However, in O'Brien's sample the length of marriage did not appear to have an effect on the amount of violence reported. Levinger's (1974) study of divorcing couples (n = 600), in Cleveland, Ohio, reported physical cruelty by 36.8% of the women and 3.3% of the men as the basis for the divorce action. Unlike O'Brien's (1971) sample Levinger's group of middle class women complained about psychological rather than physical cruelty. Levinger further noted that the lower socioeconomic class complained most frequently about money, physical cruelty, and their spouse's drinking.

Straus' (1983) study of 2,143 abuse cases suggests that although the wife beating and husband beating occur at a similar rate, 4.0 per 100, however, the wife is injured more frequently. Straus further reported that: (1) verbal abuse produces a positive correlation with physical violence, (2) education has no impact on family violence, and (3) if the husband has the final say in all decisions, high violence is three times more likely than if the husband and wife have an equal say.

American culture accepts and idolizes violence. Surveys of television (Straus, 1973), comic strips, and jokes (Steinmetz, 1978) encourage society to accept domestic violence. Straus (1979b) concluded that family violence is normatively deviant, but socially common. Although middle class values give more credence to non-violence behavioral studies indicate that violence is accepted and practiced. Straus further reported that violence is common in all classes of society. Subsequently, there is great approval for spouse and child abuse.

Spouse Abuse

Gelles's (1976) comparison of 80 families (20 from social service agencies, 20 from police reports, and 40 from the neighbors of the two combined groups) reported that the groups are not significantly different and that the more severe the violence, the more likely a wife is to seek help. Gelles concluded that if the wife is beaten daily or weekly, she calls the police and if the wife is struck at least once a month, she seeks outside help, most frequently divorce or separation. Gelles further reported that: (1) the police are called most frequently when the woman's status of education is low, (2) the abused wife most frequently was a child victim, but only 66% ever observed their parents strike one another, (3) women who have the most experience with violence, approve of violence, and (4) if the wife is employed outside the home, it denormalizes the violence and makes her more likely to seek help.

Flynn's (1977) study of abused wives (n = 33) from police records, mental health professionals, and self-reported victims found that almost all had called the police for help at one time or another. Two-thirds received counseling, one-half contacted an attorney and considered divorce and over two-thirds used emergency shelter from family or friends to protect themselves.

In Levine's (1975) study abused wives (n = 50) were asked to bring their spouses in for counseling. Levine reported that only eight men came when requested; 22 refused; and 13 agreed, but never arrived. When the children of these couples were evaluated, 71 of 114 had prior documented behavioral and medical problems. Thus, there is a limited amount of counseling that actually reaches batterers and that violent behaviors are transmitted from parents to their children.

Child Abuse

Gil's (1974) study of child abuse (n = 13,000) in the United States estimated that between 2.5 and 4.0 million injuries occurred in 1965. The reporting rate for child abuse is approximately 3.5 times greater for nonwhite populations. Silver, Dublin, and Lourie (1974) studied child abuse cases (n = 34) from medical records found that all had five-year histories of abuse. Also, Gil reported that child abuse is not restricted to a single social class or racial group, but rather it is extensive and pervasive in our society.

Blumberg's (1974) study in Nottingham, England found that 62% of the children are struck by a parent before they are one year old and 97% are struck by the time they are four years old. Steinmetz (1977a) reported that 64.8% of all child abuse is mother to child, 19.7% is parents to child, and 15.5% is father to child. The woman is more likely to injure the child. In Steinmetz's study (n = 49), 29 families used physical aggression to resolve husband-wife conflict in one week. In addition, Steinmetz (1977b) found that there is a relationship between spousal conflict and child abuse. Steinmetz concluded that violence as a problem solving method is learned in a family setting which reflects society's attitude toward physical violence.

Straus (1979a) suggests that child abuse be defined on a continuum. In Straus' study 80 parents of three- to nine-year-old children used physical punishment to train their children. Straus further reported that over 35% of 15 to 17 year old teenagers are struck by their parents in a single year, 20% of the parents who hit their children used an object, e.g., 3% used a gun or knife and 3% threatened to use a deadly weapon on their children. Straus also noted that family violence is not restricted to parents against children as three out of four children struck their brothers or sisters in a one year period.

Correlates of Domestic Violence

The exact cause of domestic violence has yet to be discovered, however, violence in the home is attributed, in varying degrees, to: alcohol (Byles, 1978; Hanks & Rosenbaum, 1977), extramarital sex (Whitehurst, 1971), power structure of a marriage (Kolb & Straus, 1974), sex roles (Sprey, 1969), sexism (Gelles, 1976; Straus, 1976), social isolation (Straus, 1979a), societal expectations of males (Toby, 1966), and verbal abuse that leads to physical abuse (Steinmetz & Straus, 1973).

Goode (1971) suggests that attraction, force, prestige, and money have been the primary powerbase of the family. Without the potential for force, the family would be less resourceful and less cohesive. Thus, violence is culturally acceptable and learned in the home.

Owens and Straus (1975) reported that violence observed, committed, or experienced in childhood is correlated with adult approval of violence. All three conditions correlate with adult approval and with interpersonal violence. In contrast, political violence does not correlate with the three childhood instances, nor does national violence. In addition, women clearly disapprove of violence more than men and experience fewer of the three childhood conditions. Straus (1979c) concluded that the family is a training ground for violence. Over 90% of parents are violent with their children, thus the concept associating violence and love is transmitted from parents to children.

Conclusions regarding police intervention in domestic disputes are seldom derived from direct observation and analysis of their activities. Frequently, research projects use nonrepresentative samples and third party surveys to draw conclusions about police intervention in domestic disputes without investigating their actual involvement.

The purpose of this study is to examine the victim-offender relationship as a determinant factor in police dispositions of domestic dispute incidents.

METHODOLOGY

Police records have been used to identify disputing families. Gelles (1972: 34-35) developed a selected sample of 20 disputing families who had police officers dispatched to their residences for disturbance calls. In addition, other families were selected by examining the police daily log to identify cases where family members initiated criminal complaints against other family members. However, the utilization of police records has limitations: first, the success of this method depends on the cooperation of police administrators and second, police logs are generally data sources of limited accuracy (Gelles, 1979: 154).

The data for this project are derived from domestic dispute and violence incidents known to police and reported monthly to the state of Ohio under the Ohio Revised Code, Domestic Dispute and Violence Program (Section 3113.32 A). These data include domestic disputes reported to Ohio police jurisdictions from August 1 through December 31, 1979 (The Ohio Report, 1980).

The police organizations (n = 607) contributing domestic dispute data represent 63% of Ohio's 971 police jurisdictions and serve 95.5% (10,284,709) of Ohio's estimated 1979 population (10,731,000: Statistical Abstracts, 1981: 12). The contributing police jurisdictions represent 60% (n = 518) of the 861 municipal and township police, 86% (n = 76) of the 88 county sheriffs, and 59% (n = 13) of the 22 special police jurisdictions in Ohio (Department of Justice, 1980: 47).

The domestic dispute and violence incidents reported to the police (n = 13,706) resulted in 3,451 criminal complaints. The initial police categorizations of the reported domestic disputes were: 740 (14%) Ohio Domestic Violence Program complaints, 536 (10%) other Ohio Revised Code complaints, and 3,875 (75%) incidents in which complaints were not initiated. The police dispositions of domestic disputes were: 1,569 (11%) arrests under the Ohio Domestic Violence Program, 829 (6%) arrests under other Ohio Revised Code violations, 2,931 (21%) referrals to other agencies, and 8,377 (61%) incidents in which the police did not take any action.

For this inquiry a "domestic dispute" is any quarrel, altercation, or strife, including domestic violence, between family or household members. "Domestic violence" occurs in domestic disputes in which a person or persons cause or attempt to cause physical harm to another family or household member. A "complaint" is a written statement or charge signed for, or filed by an officer in response to a domestic call. Complaints may be signed by family members under section 2919.25 (the Ohio Domestic Violence Program) or other sections of the Ohio Revised Code (Assault, etc).

A "family or household member" is a spouse, person living as a spouse, parent, child, or any other person related by blood or marriage who is residing or has resided with the offender. "Victims" are those family members who are identified by actual signed or filed complaints and who are subjects of domestic abuse or violence. "Complaintants" are defined as either: (1) a victim, or other "family or household member," who signs a written complaint for an officer at the time of a domestic incident; or (2) the responding law officer who himself makes a charge at the scene of a domestic dispute. "Referrals to other agencies" include counseling by police officers as well as referrals to social service agencies, prosecutors, clerk of courts, or shelter facilities (The Ohio Report, 1980: 11-12).

The domestic dispute victims are classified by their relationship to the offender (i.e., wives, husbands, mothers, fathers, children, and other family members) for comparison of victimization incidences with the initial categorization of the domestic disputes reported to the police, i.e., complaints initiated under the Ohio Domestic Violence Program, complaints initiated under other Ohio Revised Code violations, or no complaints and their subsequent handling by the police, i.e., arrest under the Ohio Domestic Violence Program, arrest under other Ohio Revised Code violations, referral to other agencies, and no action taken.

RESULTS

A computer generated random sample of police jurisdictions (n = 153) serving 25% (2,454,472) of Ohio's estimated 1979 population is the basis for the remainder of this project. The sample was generated in compliance with SPSS procedures for random (Hull & Nie, 1981: 277) and sample functions (Nie et al., 1975: 127-128). The initial categorizations of the reported domestic disputes were: 740 (14%) Ohio Domestic Violence Program criminal complaints, 536 (10%) other Ohio Revised Code violations criminal complaints, and 3,875 (75%) incidents in which criminal complaints were not initiated. The police dispositions of domestic dispute incidents were: 505 (13%) arrests under the Ohio Domestic Violence Program, 328 (6%) arrests under other Ohio Revised Code violations, 886 (17%) referrals to other agencies, and 3,432 (67%) incidents in which the police did not take any action.

Domestic dispute and violence incidents reported to the police produce a low tendency to result in criminal complaints under the Ohio Domestic Violence Program (r = .2888), a moderate tendency to result in criminal complaints under other Ohio Revised Code violations (r = .3765), and a very strong tendency not to result in criminal complaints (r = .9856) (see Table 1). Measures

Table 1

Dispute Complaint Status and Disposition

Pearson Correlation Coefficients

| | | Complaint Status | | | |
		Domestic Violence Program Complaint	Ohio Revised Code Complaint	No Complaint	Reported to Police
Disposition		n=740	n=536	n=3,875	N=5,151
		(14.4%)	(10.4%)	(75.2%)	(100%)
Domestic Violence Program Arrests	n= 505 (10%)	.8412*	.0172	.2468	.3273*
Ohio Revised Code Arrests	n= 328 (6%)	.0013	.8278*	.3883*	.4678*
Referral to Other Agencies	n= 886 (17%)	.0937	.3997*	.4135*	.4473*
No Action Taken	n=3,432 (67%)	.2287	.2450	.9771*	.9681*
Reported to Police	N=5,151 (100%)	.2888*	.3765*	.9856*	1.0000

*p<.001, two-tailed test

of association are based on .7 and above, very strong; .5 to .69, substantial; .3 to .49, moderate; .1 to .29, low; .01 to .09, negligible; and 0, no association (similar to the interpretation of Gamma developed by Davis [1971: 49]).

In domestic dispute cases where criminal complaints are initiated under the Ohio Domestic Violence Program there is a very strong tendency to arrest offenders under the Ohio Domestic Violence Program (r = .8412). In domestic dispute cases where criminal complaints are initiated under other Ohio Revised Code violations there is a very strong tendency to arrest offenders under other Ohio Revised Code violations (r = .8278) and a moderate tendency to provide referrals to other agencies (r = .3997).

In domestic dispute incidents where criminal complaints are not initiated there is a moderate tendency to arrest offenders under other Ohio Revised Code violations (r = .3883) or to provide referrals to other agencies (r = .4135) and a very strong tendency for the police not to take any action (r = .9771).

The extent of the victim's injury and their relationship to the offenders indicate that wives are victims in 69% of the domestic dispute incidents, husbands 8%, mothers 5%, fathers 2%, children 9%, and other family members 7% (see Table 2). When domestic violence occurs wives are injured or killed more frequently (35%) than are husbands (3%), mothers (2%), fathers (1%), children (5%), or other family members (3%). When injury or death occurs wives are victims more frequently (72%) than are husbands (8%), mothers (5%), fathers (3%), children (13%), or other family members (9%). Considered separately, death, occurs to wives more often than to any other victim category.

Wives, as victims, have a substantial tendency to report their domestic disputes to the police (r = .5112). Also, wives have a very strong tendency to initiate criminal complaints under the Ohio Domestic Violence Program (r = .7417) (see Table 3). In contrast husbands (r = .4007), other family members (r = .3125), and children (r = .3399) have only a moderate tendency to report their domestic victimizations to the police. Wives (r = .5908) and other family members (r = .5166) have a substantial tendency to initiate criminal complaints under other Ohio Revised Code violations. Children (r = .4965) and mothers (r = .4057) have a moderate tendency and fathers (r = .2845) and husbands (r = .2795) have a low tendency to initiate complaints under other Ohio Revised Code

Table 2

Injury Classification

	Victim-Offender Relationship						
	Wives	Husbands	Mothers	Fathers	Children	Other Family Members	total
Fatal injury	3	0	0	0	0	0	3
Nonfatal injury	540	44	27	17	70	50	748
No injury	514	80	45	19	75	55	788
	----	---	--	--	---	---	----
total	1057	124	72	36	145	105	1539

Table 3

Complaint Categorizations

Pearson Correlation Coefficients

	Victim-Offender Relationship					
	Wives	Husbands	Mothers	Fathers	Children	Other Family Members
Reported to Police	.5112*	.1645	.2072	.1721	.2042	.1824
Domestic Violence Complaints	.7417*	.4007*	.1611	.2229	.3125*	.3399*
Ohio Rev. Code Complaints	.5908*	.2795*	.4057*	.2846*	.4966*	.5166*
No Complaints	.3733*	.0871	.1462	.1173	.1111	.0814

*$p < .001$, two-tailed test

violations. In addition, there is a moderate independent tendency ($r = .3733$) for wives not to initiate criminal complaints.

In conjunction with the fact that wives tend to initiate criminal complaints more frequently than other domestic victims there is a substantial tendency for the police to arrest offenders when wives are domestic violence victims ($r = .6136$) (see Table 4).

In incidents where children ($r = .2682$) and other family members ($r = .2616$) are victims there is a low tendency to arrest offenders under the Ohio Domestic Violence Program. The cases in which wives ($r = .4976$), children ($r = .3687$), and other family members ($r = .3423$) are victims produce a moderate tendency to arrest offenders under other Ohio Revised Code violations. In cases where wives ($r = .3959$) and mothers ($r = .4092$) are victims there is a moderate tendency to provide referrals to other agencies while fathers ($r = .2908$) and children ($r = .2867$) have a low tendency for referrals. Also, in cases where wives are victims there is a moderate tendency ($r = .3799$) for the police not to take any action.

Table 4

Dispute Dispositions

Pearson Correlation Coefficients

| | Victim-Offender Relationship | | | | | |
	Wives	Husbands	Mothers	Fathers	Children	Other Family Members
Domestic Violence Arrests	.6136*	.2435	.1392	.0745	.2682*	.2616*
Ohio Rev. Code Arrests	.4976*	.1635	.1849	.1135	.3687*	.3423*
Referral to Other Agencies	.3959*	.2043	.4092*	.2908*	.2867*	.1705
No action Taken	.3799*	.1001	.1122	.1133	.0994	.1039

*$p < .001$, two-tailed test

DISCUSSION

This is a pilot study of the victim-offender relationship as a determinant factor in police dispositions of domestic dispute and violence incidents. There are limitations in this type of study. In addition, some issues are not addressed and consequently there is need for additional research in these areas, e.g., an examination of the variation in urban, suburban, and rural police dispositions of domestic dispute and violence incidents and a longitudinal study of police dispositions of domestic dispute incidents.

There are a number of strengths in this study. First, police intervention in domestic dispute and violence incidents has been an aspect of family affairs with extensive commentary, but limited research. These data are derived from reported domestic dispute incidents: (1) occurring in an extensive geographical area, (2) involving a large population, (3) randomly sampled, and (4) sampled in sufficient numbers to be considered representative of the population from which they are drawn. Second, although the findings remain to be confirmed in future research with different samples, databases, and analysis, the data reported here are generally consistent with prior research on domestic dispute and violence incidents. Finally, the population base, sample size, and methodology in this study provided insight into Ohio's police dispositions of domestic dispute and violence incidents and permits cautious generalization. From these data the following conclusions are drawn.

First, in Ohio, reported domestic dispute victims are predominantly wives (69%) and they are injured or killed in 35% of these incidents. In general, wives are domestic dispute victims significantly more frequently than husbands, mothers, fathers, children, and other family or household members. Considered separately, fatal and nonfatal injury occurs to wives more frequently than to any other victim category. Mothers are injured more frequently than fathers, but less often than children. Also, in domestic disputes where no injury occurs there is substantially more victimization of wives than husbands. In fact, wives are victims more frequently than all other victim categories combined.

Second, considered independently, 67% of the domestic dispute incidents reported to the police do not result in any official action being taken, i.e., by the police. In consideration of the fact that domestic dispute victims are predominantly wives the implications of police inaction in domestic disputes are clear and support the findings of Parnas (1967: 929) and Straus, Gelles, and Steinmetz (1980: 233), i.e., by their failure to take definitive action the police condone husbands assaulting their wives. Consequently, the wife's right to protection is diminished by the police system's unwillingness to cope with domestic violence.

Third, although criminal complaints are initiated in 25% of the domestic dispute incidents reported to the police, offenders are arrested in only 16% of these incidents. These data suggest that the police do not arrest as many offenders as are justified by victim initiated criminal complaints and there is a strong indication that police do not initiate criminal complaints in domestic violence cases of their own volition.

Fourth, these data tend to disagree with the findings of Black (1971: 1097) and Cumming, Cumming, and Edell (1965: 281), i.e., the police are more likely to arrest strangers rather than intimate family members involved in disturbances. These data suggest the reverse: in the specific instances (although few in number) when wives are the victims (rather than peripheral family or household members) *and* initiate criminal complaints the highest incidence of offender arrests are recorded.

In summary, domestic dispute and violence incidents where wives initiate criminal complaints produce the strongest tendency to result in the offender's arrest. Clearly, in those specific domestic violence incidents where criminal complaints are initiated, the order of victim priority associated with their dispositions is: (1) wives, (2) children, (3) husbands, (4) fathers, (5) other family or household members, and (6) mothers.

In addition, there are other aspects of domestic dispute and violence incidents where tentative conclusions can be reached. First, due to a misinterpretation by police, that domestic violence is a noncriminal event, combined with their traditional "hands off" approach to civil complaints, domestic dispute victims who do not initiate criminal complaints do not receive adequate protection or services from the criminal justice system.

Second, the few cases where wives initiate criminal complaints produce significantly more arrest or referral activity than when other family or household members are victims. Thus, it is a distinct advantage for the domestic violence victim, i.e., the wife, who desires that the police take definitive action on her behalf, file a criminal complaint and insist that appropriate police action be initiated to protect her rights to be free from physical assault. Although, victims filing criminal complaints with the police at the scene of a violent domestic dispute will not guarantee an offender's arrest, there is unmistakable evidence that a formal complaint will be a strong motivator for the police and provide direction toward an arrest as an end result to domestic violence.

Finally, the Ohio Domestic Violence Program which is intended to enable and encourage police officers to arrest domestic violence offenders on their own volition, without the prerequisite of a criminal complaint initiated at the scene by the victim, clearly has not been effective. Thus, a preliminary assessment of the effectiveness and value of Ohio's Domestic Violence Program can be formulated.

The legislative intent of authorizing expanded police discretion and arrest powers in domestic dispute and violence incidents, specifically to enable the police to be more active/effective in arresting offenders and provide more assistance/protection to the victims, has been thwarted by the police system's lack of ability, interest, or willingness to protect the victim's (i.e., the wife's) right to be free from physical assault.

REFERENCES

Black, D. (1971). The social organization of arrest. *Stanford Law Review, 23,* 1087-1111.

Blumberg, M. (1974). When parents hit out. In S.K. Steinmetz and M.A. Straus (eds.), *Violence in the family.* (pp. 148-150). New York: Harper and Row.

Byles, J.A. (1978). Violence, alcohol problems and other problems in disintegrating families. *Journal of Studies on Alcohol, 39,* 551-553.

Cumming, E., Cumming, I. & Edell, L. (1965). Policemen as philosopher, guide, and friend. *Social Problems, 12*(3), 276-286.

Davis, J.A. (1971). *Elementary survey analysis.* Englewood Cliffs, NJ: Prentice-Hall.

Department of Justice (1980). *Justice agencies in the United States: Summary report 1980.* Washington, DC: Bureau of Justice Statistics, U.S. Government Printing.

Flynn, J.P. (1977). Recent findings related to wife abuse. *Social Casework, 58,* 13-20.

Gaquin, D.A. (1978). Spouse abuse: Data from the national crime survey. *Victimology, 2,* 632-643.

Gelles, R.J. (1972). *The violent home: A study of physical aggression between husbands and wives.* Beverly Hills, CA: Sage.

Gelles, R.J. (1976). Abused wives: Why do they stay? *Journal of Marriage and the Family, 38,* 659-668.

Gelles, R.J. (1979). *Family violence.* Beverly Hills, CA: Sage.

Gil, D.G. (1971). Violence against children. *Journal of Marriage and the Family, 33,* 637-648.

Goode, W.J. (1971). Force and violence in the family. *Journal of Marriage and the Family, 33,* 624-636.

Hanks, S.E. & Rosenbaum, C.P. (1977). Battered women: A study of women who live with violent alcohol-abusing men. *American Journal of Orthopsychiatry, 47,* 291-306.

Kolb, T.M. & Straus, M.A. (1974). Marital power and marital happiness in relation to problem-solving ability. *Journal of Marriage and the Family, 36,* 756-766.

Hull, C.H. & Nie, N.H. (1981). *SPSS update 7-9: New procedures and facilities for releases 7-9*. New York: McGraw-Hill.

Levine, M.B. (1975). Interparental violence and its effect on the children: A study of 50 families in general practice. *Medical Science and the Law, 15*, 172-176.

Levinger, G. (1974). Physical abuse among applicants for divorce. in S.K. Steinmetz & M.A. Straus (eds.), *Violence in the Family*. (pp. 85-88). New York: Harper and Row.

Nie, N.H., Hull, C.H., Jenkins, J.G., Steinbrenner, K. & Bent, D.H. (1975). *SPSS: Statistical package for the social sciences*. New York: McGraw-Hill.

O'Brien, J.E. (1971). Violence in divorce-prone families. *Journal of Marriage and the Family, 33*, 692-698.

Owens, D.M. & Straus, M.A. (1975). The social structure of violence in childhood and approval of violence as an adult. *Aggressive Behavior, 1*, 193-211.

Parnas, R.I. (1967). The police response to the domestic disturbance. *Wisconsin Law Review, 1967*(4), 914-960.

Sprey, J. (1969). On the management of conflict in families. *Journal of Marriage and the Family, 33*, 722-731.

Statistical abstracts of the United States 1980. (1981). Department of Commerce, U.S. Government Printing.

Steinmetz, S.K. (1977a). *Cycle of violence: Assertive, aggressive and abusive family interaction*. New York: Praeger.

Steinmetz, S.K. (1977b). The use of force for resolving family conflict: The training ground for abuse. *The Family Coordinator, 26*, 19-26.

Steinmetz, S.K. (1978). The battered husband syndrome. *Victimology, 2*, 499-509.

Steinmetz, S.K. & Straus, M.A. (1973). The family as cradle of violence. *Society, 710*, 50-56.

Straus, M.A. (1973). A general systems theory approach to a theory of violence between family members. *Social Science Information, 12*, 105-125.

Straus, M.A. (1974). Leveling, civility, and violence in the family. *Journal of Marriage and the Family, 36*, 13-29.

Straus, M.A. (1976). Sexual inequality, cultural norms, and wife beating. *Victimology, 1*, 543-559.

Straus, M.A. (1977). Societal morphogenesis and intrafamily violence in cross-cultural perspectives. *Annals of the New York Academy of Sciences, 285*, 717-730.

Straus, M.A. (1979a). Family patterns and child abuse in a nationally representative American sample. *Child Abuse and Neglect, 3*, 213-255.

Straus, M.A. (1979b). Measuring intrafamily conflict and violence: The Conflict Tactics (CT) scales. *Journal of Marriage and the Family, 41*, 75-88.

Straus, M.A. (1979c). A sociological perspective on the causes of family violence. In M.R. Green (ed.), *Violence and the American Family*. (pp. 7-31). Washington, DC: AAS.

Straus, M.A. (1983). Ordinary violence, child abuse, and wife beating: What do they have in common? In D. Finkelhor, R.J. Gelles, G.T. Hotaling & M.A.

Straus (eds.), *The dark side of families: Current family violence research*. (pp. 213-234). Beverly Hills, CA: Sage.

Straus, M.A., Gelles, R. & Steinmetz, S.K. (1980). *Behind closed doors: Violence in the American family*. Garden City, NY: Anchor.

The Ohio report on domestic violence 1979 (1980). Columbus, OH: Attorney General of Ohio.

Toby, J. (1966). Violence and masculine ideal: Some qualitative data. *Annuals of the American Academy of Political Social Science, 345*, 19-28.

Whitehurst, R.N. (1971). Violence potential in extramarital sexual responses. *Journal of Marriage and the Family, 33*, 683-691.

Parental Discipline
and Criminal Deviance

Michael W. H. Len

INTRODUCTION

Much has been assumed about a causal relationship between harsh and abusive punishment by parents and the criminal activity of their children. Past studies, however, only briefly dealt with whether criminals themselves perceived this, or had specifically used the parental punishment they had received as children to excuse their own responsibility for illegal acts. Such an examination is made in this article. Data is analyzed from in-depth interviews conducted with 63 adult inmates of correctional facilities. The findings regarding their opinions of connection between parental punishment and adult offender status are not consistent with the stereotype of criminal behavior and attitude as well as the results of some past research. Several suggestions are made to explain this phenomenon and call attention to certain parental behaviors and expectations.

LITERATURE REVIEW

There is much evidence to show the extensive use of physical punishment by parents of their children. Steinmetz's (1977) sample of 78 people between the ages of 18 and 30 contained close to 70% who could remember physical punishment being imposed on them by their parents. Gelles' (1977) national probability sample of over 1000 families produced information about the incidence of parent-to-child violence within their family unit. An act which was in-

Michael W. H. Len is Director of Family Services, Naval Air Station, Barbers Point, HI 96862; and Adjunct Professor of Social Work, University of Hawaii.

tended to injure a person physically was classified as violence; 73% of his respondents could attest to at least one such occurrence in their family during 1975.

A scientifically-selected representative sample of 2200 children were questioned about their home environment in a study by the Foundation for Child Development (1977), with nearly two-thirds revealing that they were spanked. Data from the Louis Harris survey (cited in Stark & McEvoy, 1970) are relevant. The poll consisted of over 1000 interviews with a representative national sample of adult Americans. The respondents said that as children, 93% of them were given spankings. Almost 85% had themselves spanked a child. Today in America a child is not necessarily considered sacrosanct and exempt from "injury," "beating," and "spankings" — terms which are used in the studies quoted above to connote the physical use of force employed by parents on their children.

Against this background of known violence in families, whether or not in the name of discipline, have been the issues of whether violence-begets-violence and whether those who were abused as children stand a greater chance of becoming aggressive and antisocial adults. There has been some investigation into the childrearing history of those who are obviously violent, i.e., persons identified by treatment professionals as aggressive and dangerous to society. There has been research into the physical punishment and abusive treatment by parents of juvenile delinquents (McCord, McCord & Zola, 1959; Welsh, 1976).

A study by Easson and Steinhilber (1961) indicated the extent of influence parents have on the conduct of violence by their children. It investigated case histories of eight children in which one or both parents had actually condoned or unconsciously encouraged murderous assaults on themselves, their spouses, or other family members. In two of these eight cases brutal beatings by the father were recorded; in a third, the beatings were meted out by the mother.

Palmer's study (cited in Steinmetz & Straus, 1974) into the psychology of murderers revealed that those studied experienced more actual beatings, not just spankings, from their parents when compared to their siblings. Duncan, Frazier, Litin, Johnson, and Barron

(1958) found that in four of the childhood histories of six murderers they had studied, the one significant common feature was the "continuous, remorseless brutality" inflicted by a parent.

In addition to these studies, which intentionally examined samples of criminals, biographies or autobiographies of offenders mention the prevalence of harsh physical discipline in their early lives (Linder, 1944; Evans, 1960). This is not to say, of course, that all who have been physically punished by parents grow up to become violent and antisocial. It is further documented that a great number of these lives of crime were preceded by childhoods filled with abusive and physically severe treatment at the hands of parents and caregivers.

Duncan et al. (1958) commented that their "prisoners showed a surprising degree of insight in relating their criminal violence to their family experiences." Their opinion of culpability for the homicides, however, as it related to the parental treatment was not studied. Yochelson and Samenow (1976) mentioned that the criminal tends to make "himself the victim of unreasonable, punitive parents," especially when justifying what he had done wrong. They reported that "when criminals account to others for violations, they seek exoneration by claiming to be victims of their environment . . . the broken home, the drinking father, and so forth."

Past studies, however, did not specifically examine whether those criminals used parental punishment as excuses to minimize responsibility for their own illegal acts. Parent-blaming is an important issue to rehabilitation and treatment professionals in their work with this particular group of people. It is also relevant to parents as they contemplate disciplinary alternatives in the raising of their children. This study, therefore, sought to clarify whether criminals do connect their adult offenses with the punishment meted out by their parents.

METHODOLOGY

Interviews of 63 male and female prisoners were conducted in San Francisco County Jails and the Hawaii State Prison in Honolulu. Selection was based on the individual's willingness to answer several open-ended questions asked of all the subjects regarding

their parents' disciplinary techniques. They were told that no reward was forthcoming for participation in the interviews.

The mean age of the sample of 52 males and 11 females was 27.5
years. The mean educational attainment was 10.5 years of school-
ing. Crimes against persons, such as murder, rape, and assault,
were committed by 44, or 70%. The remaining subjects were incarcerated for property crimes, e.g., auto theft, forgery, etc.

The severity and frequency of corporal punishment inflicted on
the subjects ranged from "none" to "severe physical abuse." Two
(3%) of the subjects stated that they did not receive any corporal
punishment. The others were categorized into three groups depending on maximal parental punishment received.

(1) *Mild Punishment* ($N = 10$ % = 16) was the occasional and
brief slapping of the extremities or the buttocks with the hand. Subjects in this category reported that no other form of punishment was
received.

(2) *Harsh Punishment* ($N = 26$ % = 41) was the striking of the
body with a belt, slipper, switch, ruler-like item, length of rope, or
electrical cord. The slapping of the face with an open palm is also in
this category. A parent who employed Harsh Punishment did so as a
regular means of discipline. To be included in this category, the
subject had to indicate that Harsh Punishment was used more than
once.

(3) *Violent Abuse* ($N = 25$ % = 40) was that practice involving the
use of unlikely disciplinary instruments by an adult on a child. Such
objects give rise to the theory that commensurate discipline was not
the intention and further obedience was not the desire, but that terror and the mere infliction of pain might have been the aim of the
parent. Reported were the use of knives, pipes, iron rods, hammers,
rocks, broom handles, boards, 2×4s (pieces of thick lumber),
chains, hangers, belt buckles, pins, rubber hoses, telephones, pots,
pans, bowling pins, and pool sticks. Also included were the following actions: banging of the child's head on immovable objects, attempting to drown, burning, punching with fists to the face or vis-
cera, choking, and inserting of noxious substances in the mouth.
Only one such incident involving any of the items or actions was
necessary for a subject to be listed as a recipient of Violent Abuse.
Many of the 25 in this category were violently abused more than
once.

RESULTS

Table I gives combined responses to the question regarding whether, in the opinion of the subject, there is a connection between his childhood punishment and his adult crime which brought him to prison.

"Yes," There Is a Connection

All 12 subjects who believe that there is a connection between the way their parents punished them and their criminality received Harsh Punishment or Violent Abuse. Comments by several of these individuals follow:

> I blame my mother for the trouble I'm in. . . . It was her fault, she belongs in here, not me.

> My stepfather has a lot to do with my being here. He pulled some mean kind of stuff; everything. I knew what I was going to get everyday — lickings.

> All these things (Violent Abuse) were happening to me and I was trying to get revenge (through crimes).

TABLE I

CHILDHOOD PUNISHMENT AND ADULT CRIMES

Is there a Connection?

Type of Physical Punishment	Response					
	"YES"		"UNSURE"		"NO"	
	n	%	n	%	n	%
NO PHYSICAL	0	0	0	0	2	5
MILD PUNISHMENT	0	0	1	17	9	20
HARSH PUNISHMENT	5	42	2	33	19	42
VIOLENT ABUSE	7	58	3	50	15	33
N=63	12		6		45	

"Unsure" Whether There Is a Connection

Six subjects were not able to express an opinion regarding parental responsibility for their crimes. Five of these six received the two most severe forms of punishment at the hands of their parents. A typical response follows:

> I don't know if there's a connection. I don't want to tell you "yes" or "no." I'm not too good at putting all the pieces together to find out the account, like that.

"No," There Is No Connection

There were 45 subjects who do not connect their parents' method of punishment with their crimes. Harsh Punishment and Violent Abuse were inflicted on 75% of these subjects. Here are some comments:

> No, it's my own thing, I cannot blame my parents on that.

> I think it was all my part. I didn't know who I was, where I was going.

Responses sometimes took on the tone of downgrading those who did blame parents. Certain individuals apparently feel that to censure parents is to deny that one is responsible for one's own actions.

> Everybody puts it off on their folks. I knew when I was doing wrong even when I knew I could get away with it. I can't really blame my parents for what I did. That's a cop out.

> I could never blame my parents for where I am. Some do, but it's not my trip.

The two subjects whose parents did not physically punish them report that they do not feel this lack of corporal punishment contributed to the commission of their crimes. Here are their comments:

My parents were OK. They brought us up all right. . . . My parents have no responsibility for this. I really don't know how things could have been better.

No, there is no connection for me; my relationship with my parents, like I say, is the best any parents could do.

DISCUSSION

A large majority of this study's sample made no connection between their childhood punishment and their subsequent offender status. Another finding was that severity of parental punishment did not necessarily influence its use as an excuse for criminality. More who received Harsh Punishment or Violent Abuse did not feel there was a connection, i.e., 34, than did, i.e., 12.

There are several reasons for some subjects to respond "yes," there is a connection, and for others to respond "no," there is no connection, even though they all may have received the same type of punishment, i.e., Harsh Punishment or Violent Abuse.

The traditional adage of "doing your own time" extends to accepting the fact that actions which brought a person to prison were entirely of his own doing. Prisoners are discouraged from developing reasons for their illegal behavior which relate to their parents' treatment of them, in spite of the fact that on occasion some psychiatrically-unsophisticated prisoners have shown a "surprising degree of insight in relating their criminal violence to their family experiences" (Duncan et al. 1958). It is quite possible, therefore, that this belief system of denying parental responsibility was operating and influencing the responses of these subjects who say they do not believe that there is a connection between the crimes they committed and the parental punishment they received.

Another factor which may have been at work to forestall blame by these 45 subjects is the almost intuitive feeling that one is supposed to love his parents. This injunction is not supposed to involve conditional affection, contingent on how one is treated. The following quote is an appropriate illustration: "I love my mother; I love my father . . . even though they beat me."

The feeling of guilt may have been in operation for some subjects when asked whether there was a connection. They may have realized that they deserved punishment for certain of their misbehaviors. Therefore, the knowledge that the punishment was harsh, even abusive, would be irrelevant. In spite of the severity of the treatment, they could have simply denied that any of their parents' actions were connected to their subsequent offenses. An observation by one of the subjects is applicable:

> Maybe there are guilt feelings. Maybe it (Violent Abuse) was justified in a few cases, even though it may have been extreme. Maybe basically they know the parents are trying to convince them they did wrong. "The parents are always right" kind of thing.

Another explanation for subjects' denial that their parents' punishment and abuse of them relates to their crimes may involve the sense of physical power and strength which is so fervently sought by prisoners. Manocchio and Dunn (1970) report on the significance of individual musculature and the emphasis on weightlifting and bodybuilding inside prisons. The macho feeling is prevalent, and involves both male and female inmates. To admit, therefore, that one succumbed to the physical retribution of a parent, and to blame that parent, might be personally embarrassing to many in the criminal subculture. Two subjects have observations:

> They feel pride that they were punched by their fathers and stood up to them. No one else can punch as hard as dad.

The other comments on his own background:

> Why should I be scared of others? No one can hit me harder than my old man.

Still another factor which may have been at work to enhance this denial that the abusive parents are responsible for the subjects' crimes is what Gelles (1977) calls "victimblaming." The victim of familial abuse blames himself for having incurred the parental wrath, and therefore deserved to be hit or needed to be hit. The victim may feel this even though his provocation may have been as nondescript as having been in the wrong place at the wrong time, e.g., in the presence of a parent in a bad mood.

He might also blame himself for the abuse based on the philosophy that he "belongs" to the parent; he is "their" child. Thereafter, any use of the abusive treatment as an excuse for subsequent illegal behavior would create internal dissonance and hence be avoided. Button (1975) found this phenomenon occurring between teenage boys and their parents in his study of felonious and delinquent behavior. Regardless of the severity or the incommensurate nature of the punishment, the boys defended their parents and almost always indicated that they deserved the punishment received.

SUMMARY

Only two subjects in the sample of 63 reported that they were not punished physically. Over 40% were struck with objects or on the face, and a like number received mistreatment of a magnitude which was categorized as Violent Abuse. Those who made no connection between the punishment they received from parents and their subsequent offender status consisted primarily of the harshly punished and violently abused.

Some primary reasons for subjects to deny that parents' punitive actions precipitated their crimes are the prison system's admonishment to assume responsibility for one's own wrongdoing; the subjects' acceptance of blame for having incurred the parental wrath; the subject's feeling that parents deserve unconditional affection; and the feelings that if they were deserving of parental punishment, the severity of that punishment is irrelevant.

The study's contradiction of the conventional wisdom, as well as other research and case studies, that offenders blame parents and upbringing for their criminal careers justifies the need for future research to explore this area more extensively. A larger sample with an equal number of subjects in each punishment category could be interviewed. More certainty could then be given any assumption regarding differences in proportion among those who were punished similarly, but who have different opinions about a connection between that punishment and their adult crimes.

It is a hopeful finding, nonetheless, that the majority in this sample did not attribute their crimes to an antecedent such as parental punishment, a factor which some parents are not eager or equipped to change. That offenders realize their criminality can be examined in the present without resort to blaming a past variable is significant to the areas of parent education, therapy, and research.

REFERENCES

Button, A., "Some antecedents of felonious and delinquent behavior." *Journal of Clinical Child Psychology*, 1975, *2*, (3), 35-37.

Duncan, G.M., Frazier, S.H., Litin, E.M., Johnson, A.M. & Barron, A.J., "Etiological factors in first-degree murder." *Journal of the American Medical Association*, 1958, 168, 1755-1758.

Easson, W.M. & Steinhilber, R.M., "Murderous aggression by children and adolescents." *Archives of General Psychiatry*, 1961, *4*, 27-35.

Evans, J., *Three Men: An Experiment in the Biography of Emotion*. New York: Alfred A. Knopf, 1960.

Foundation for Child Development, *Summary of Preliminary Results, National Survey of Children*. New York: Foundation for Child Development, March 1977.

Gelles, R.J., *Violence towards Children in the United States*. Durham, NH: University of New Hampshire Press, 1977.

Lindner, R.M., *Rebel without a Cause: The Hypnoanalysis of a Criminal Psychopath*. New York: Grune & Stratton, 1944.

McCord, W., McCord, J. & Zola, I.K., *Origins of Crime: A New Evaluation of the Cambridge-Somerville Youth Study*. New York: Columbia University Press, 1959.

Manocchio, A.J. & Dunn, J., *The Time Game*. Beverly Hills, CA: Sage Publications, 1970.

Stark, R. & McEvoy, J., "Middle-class violence." *Psychology Today*, November 1970, pp. 52-54, 110-112.

Steinmetz, S., "The use of force for resolving family conflict: The training ground for abuse." *Family Coordinator*, 1977, *26*, 19-26.

Steinmetz, S. & Straus, M.S. (eds.), *Violence in the Family*. New York: Dodd, Mead, & Co., 1974.

Welsh, R.S., "Severe parental punishment and discipline: A developmental theory." *Journal of Clinical Child Psychology*, 1976, *3* (1), 11-21.

Yochelson, S. & Samenow, S.E., *The Criminal Personality: A Profile for Change*. New York: Jason Aronson, 1976.

Juvenile Prostitution:
A Critical Perspective

Terrence Sullivan

If you happen to be rich and you feel like a night's
entertainment,
You can pay for a gay escapade.
If you happen to be rich and alone and you need a
companion,
You can ring-ting-aling for the maid.

Ebb and Kander
"Money, Money" from Cabaret

INTRODUCTION

Everywhere these days, the popular press is speaking about the
unspeakable. The media are replete with commentary on the sexual
behavior of families and youth. Rush's (1980) "best kept secret" of
child sexual abuse has become a public concern. In the U.S.A.,
congressional hearings on the protection of children from sexual
exploitation through juvenile prostitution and pornography have
generated a flurry of research studies (Weisberg, 1985; Young,
1978). In Canada, federal concern regarding the sexual exploitation
of young persons has resulted in two very recent reports. The *Report of the Committee on Sexual Offences Against Children and
Youths* (1984), hereafter known as the Badgley Report, details a
range of original and secondary research and suggests a large num-

Terrence Sullivan is Senior Policy Advisor, Children's Unit, Ministry of Community and Social Services; and Adjunct Professor of Sociology, York University, Toronto, Ontario, M5B 1L2.

ber of specific social and legal reforms designed to afford better protection to sexually exploited young persons. The *Report of the Special Committee on Pornography and Prostitution* (1985), hereafter known as the Fraser Report, while focusing primarily on adults, also proposes a large number of specific reform and protection amendments relevant to young people.

The Canadian studies, as well as earlier American counterparts, represent epic pieces of medico-legal discourse and are enormously intimidating. In examining the data crossing medical, legal, sociological and psychological frameworks, informed criticism becomes an onerous task. To speak critically about a subject as sacrosanct as the protection of children from sexual exploitation risks public outrage and professional ostracism. Yet it is precisely the obvious expertise, the apparent humanism and classlessness in the conduct of such studies which beg for critical inquiry.

The paper focuses on juvenile prostitution for two reasons. The current flurry of proposed Canadian legislative activity related to juvenile prostitution and sexual consent is the first reason. Secondly, juvenile prostitution represents the intersection of three important institutions of sexuality: the family, prostitution, and the free market economy.

The central argument of this paper is that much of contemporary discourse follows from an historic pattern of regulating family life through prescription and proscription on sexual behavior. Contemporary medico-legal discourses on sexuality grant authority to certain professional classes while reinforcing an essentially conservative biopolitical economy mediated through the agencies of the liberal welfare state (O'Neill, 1985). This is rarely clearer than in the case of juvenile prostitution. The pattern develops by pathologizing "disturbed" family relations and offering up state sanctioned and mandated legal/therapeutic interventions designed to restore "healthy," normative, familial sexuality. These professional arguments popularized in psychiatric, social work, and child care literature define a certain "regime of truth" and play down or ignore much of the biopolitical economy surrounding juvenile prostitution (Foucault, 1978). Needless to say, intervention strategies generally ignore this economy and focus on individuals and families as repositories of blame and points of intervention.

A few caveats are worth mentioning. The existence of real socio-sexual problems such as rape, sexual assault, and family violence are not at issue here. Nor is the intention to argue that an individual's constitutional and psychological history do not play important roles in juvenile prostitution. Rather, the intention is to focus on the way this phenomenon is popularly portrayed and regulated in the context of the family and the economy. These explorations are intended, in the spirit of Foucault (1978, 1979, 1980), to look at the development of prohibitions, specialized knowledges, and their links to certain social groups. The intention is not to unmask all dominant, socially ratified discourse on child sexuality as ideological instruments of oppression. Concern over the safety of children is real, and steps to protect children from harm generally do improve their safety.

The lines of inquiry follow three related subthemes. First, Canadian legislative history is reviewed in the context of a number of the social forces at work. Secondly, the economic and market forces affecting prostitution are looked at from a number of related dimensions. Thirdly, the role of the state in regulating families is commented upon in the context of enhanced children's rights.

THE LAW AND JUVENILE PROSTITUTION

The particularly Canadian focus of this paper follows from the author's familiarity with Canadian sources and legislation. Detailed information on recent American legislative activity can be found in Weisberg (1985).

The legislative history of prostitution in Canada is well documented in the report of the Canadian Advisory Council on the Status of Women (1984) entitled *Prostitution in Canada*. The earliest Canadian legislation enacted in lower Canada in 1839 grew out of vagrancy statutes designed to move undesirables from the street and arrest inmates of bawdy houses. A Canadian clone of the 1864 English *Contagious Diseases Act* was enacted in 1865. This legislation was created by a lobby of upper class doctors, military officers and politicians and was intended to regulate the necessary evil of prostitution by minimizing the effects of venereal disease.

In England, following the enactment, a massive campaign was

mounted by Josephine Butler to repeal the legislation on grounds of discrimination. The argument was raised that the regulation presupposed a supply of women motivated largely by poverty, drawn from the working classes, and subjected them alone to police harassment on streets of designated towns. The English controversy generated 500 books and pamphlets, 20,000 petitions, 900 public meetings and took until 1886 to repeal (Nield, 1973). The Canadian version of the statute expired unceremoniously, while the debate on whether or not to regulate or license followed, on a quieter scale, the English debate. Early Canadian legislation aimed at prohibiting all persons from procuring the defilement of women under 21 years by false pretenses was enacted in 1869. International concern over the scandal of child prostitution and white slavery resulted in public pressure to afford greater protection to girls and women.

In 1886 in Canada a piece of legislation entitled *Offences Against Public Morals and Public Inconvenience* prohibited householders from allowing women under 16 to reside for purposes of prostitution. The legislation also made it an offence to entice women to prostitute or to seduce any girl of previously chaste character between 12 and 16 years of age. The *Criminal Code* of 1892 made it unlawful for parents or guardians to encourage the defilement of their charges and conspiracy to defile was created as an offence. This legislation moved from the regulating effect of earlier Acts to a prohibitive function in an attempt to eradicate prostitution.

Between 1840 and 1900 the Toronto Goal register showed that the majority of people convicted under these acts were prostitutes who "were financially impoverished, generally illiterate, frequently immigrant, and overwhelmingly female" (C.A.C.S.W., 1984, p.12). The profiteers, procurers, madams, and property owners were rarely prosecuted. Attempts at prohibition were unlikely to succeed when directed at prostitutes, the least powerful players in the prostitution game.

Early legislation aimed at rehabilitation or reform logically focused on children. A rash of early child protection statutes were enacted at the turn of the century to remove young girls from the custody of their parents where the parents indulged in sexual behavior of a socially unacceptable manner in the home. Girls were apprehended and transferred to the newly established industrial refuges. The rehabilitative approach legislated plans to rescue and reform prostitutes and train children so they would never enter the ranks of prostitution. This thrust had the effect, in certain jurisdictions, of special programs and prisons being set up and the serving of longer prison terms in the name of rehabilitating women. Indeed, these rehabilitative approaches, promoted by middle and upper class women advocates on the argument that hookers were blameless for their condition, sometimes resulted in greater discrimination. It was working class and immigrant families who found their children apprehended, and it was again the working class prostitutes who served terms in the new women's prisons.

In 1972, the vagrancy section of the *Criminal Code* was repealed in favor of prohibiting soliciting in a public place. A series of interpretations on soliciting in a public place ended in the Supreme Court ruling in *Hutt vs. The Queen* (1978) that soliciting be "pressing and persistent." There was a flurry of municipal bylaws passed, challenged in the provincial courts of Quebec and Alberta, and finally, in *Westendorp vs. The Queen* (1983), those bylaws dealing directly with prostitution were declared *ultra vires* or overstepping jurisdiction. This currently leaves the issue of prostitution within federal jurisdiction.

The *Hutt* and *Westendorp* decisions are seen by many, including police, as the chief contributing factors to the increase in the street trade. Municipal bylaws, although expensive and awkward to enforce, did dramatically reduce visible prostitution. Moreover, the enforcement of the bylaws showed that the people who were getting most of the charges were the hookers, not the clients, even though clients were chargeable under the bylaws in some jurisdictions.

The Badgley Report (1984) recommends criminalizing juvenile prostitution for both hookers and their clients with severe sanctions on pimps. Amongst other recommendations, publicizing the names of clients is suggested as a kind of modern-day *charivari* or public humiliation (Shorter, 1975). The Fraser Report (1985) suggests a strengthening of sanctions against customers of juvenile prostitutes as well as strengthened sanctions against pimping and procuring.

Until now, Canadian law as it affects juvenile prostitution has historically been uneven and discriminatory both in its spirit and its enforcement, essentially punishing rather than protecting, without significantly affecting those who benefit from prostitution.

THE NETHER ECONOMY
OF JUVENILE PROSTITUTION

Questions on the economy of prostitution, who benefits, and which services exchange on which markets, have occupied many commentators. In fact, much of the great nineteenth century debate by social reformers concerned the economic motivation for prostitution. The contemporary spiral of this debate has arisen because of the visibility and scale of prostitution and its effect on local markets. While there are certainly residents who are simply harassed and morally offended by the activities of street prostitution, much of the public pressure arises from fears over property values and business activity. In jurisdictions where juvenile prostitution is good for business, such as Thailand and the Philippines, prostitution flourishes. In those jurisdictions there are plenty of local pressures to allow an unfettered free market approach to prostitution. In 1977, for example, about 1,000 men from Germany alone went to Thailand on sex included package tours ("Tourism and Prostitution," 1979).

If we move to examine who actually trades and exchanges through prostitution beyond the client and prostitute, there are many who actually benefit from this market. There are those who profit directly, such a pimps and owners of bawdy houses and certain hotels. There are other supporting players including some bellhops, taxi drivers, police, lawyers, social workers, and doctors and health care workers who all profit indirectly in the course of their work. The role of helping professionals will be further developed below.

The question of economic inducements to prostitution was a big part of the nineteenth century debates. In Parent-Duchatelet's classic and comprehensive survey on the habits and health of nineteenth century Parisian prostitutes he comments:

Of all the causes of prostitution in Paris, and probably in all great towns, there are none more influential than the want of work, and indigence resulting from insufficient earning. What are the earnings of our hairdressers, our seamstresses, our milliners? Compare the wages of the most skillful with those of the more ordinary and moderately able, and we shall see if it be possible for these latter to procure even the strict necessities of life (cited in Nield, 1973, p.460).

In the nineteenth century debates, prostitution circulated in *lumpenproletariat* culture, part of the fabric of life of the urban poor, the victims of an uncertain economy "frequently unemployed and always underpaid, continuously disadvantaged in a social system which equated profit with virtue and poverty with personal inadequacy . . . " (Nield, 1973, p.8).

Today, in North America few people wish to acknowledge any real link between the youth unemployment rate and juvenile prostitution. In the contemporary liberal welfare state, it is argued, there are sufficient social programs to meet the basic needs of the unemployed and the disadvantaged. Twentieth century inner cities have travelled far from the cities of the Victorian period when a surplus of families and individuals flocked to the industrial cities looking for work and poverty, disease and destitution were indeed grave and abundant. Achieving even a subsistence-level existence was truly difficult. In the modern welfare state, subsistence through social programs is quite possible, but one must have the knowledge, motivation, and tenacity necessary to access social welfare assistance.

Are there significant economic and labor market-based incentives for juveniles to prostitute? In the few existing Canadian studies it is commonly observed that young prostitutes have poor education and few marketable skills:

They often did not have social insurance cards, drivers license, health care cards or credit ratings. All of these take time, money and knowledge that a young or poorly educated person on the edges of a welfare system often lacks (C.A.C.S.W., 1984, p.43).

In the Badgley Report's (1984) sample of 229 juvenile prostitutes of both sexes, the median educational attainment was grade 10 and most of the young people had no desire to continue their formal education. Of the young people interviewed in the Badgley study, about 80% of the females and 63% of the males had no other form of employment at the time they were interviewed. For those with other forms of employment, the jobs were typically low-skill, low-wage positions as waiters, cashiers, ice cream vendors, kitchen helpers, and housekeepers. This is reminiscent of the findings of an early American study of prostitution. At the turn of the century in the city of New York, two of three classes of hookers were described:

> In the first place there is a large class of women—foundlings and orphans and the offspring of the unusually poor—without training, mental or moral, they remain ignorant and disagreeable, slovenly and uncouth, good for nothing in the social and economic organism. . . . In many cities there are great classes of women without any resources except their earnings as needlewomen, day-workers, domestics, or factory hands. A season of nonemployment presents them with the alternatives of starvation or prostitution. These form the "occasional prostitutes" who, according to Blaschko, far outweigh all others in the city of Berlin ("The Social Evil," cited in *Prostitution in America*, 1976, p.9).

In the Badgley Report (1984) about 40% of the young people regarded street prostitution as a full-time job, about 25% as a part-time job, and about 30% saw it as occasional work. About 65% worked on the street at least 4 days a week. (There is a very detailed analysis of time and work patterns in chapter 45 of Badgley's Report.) Average gross daily earnings for most of the young male prostitutes were $140.85; for the females, $215.49. For the females, this sum annualizes out to about $40,000 based on a four day work week and six weeks holiday per year. This figure is impressive. Only about 10% of Badgley's young female hookers reported having a current pimp, although close to 40% reported having had a pimp in the past and where active, the pimp generally took most of the earnings. This impressive income figure should be considered as income from the low end of the skill range in the market scale.

Although little is known about real annual incomes from the up-market work involved in massage parlors, private clubs, escort and beeper services, the income appears to be somewhat better, and working conditions are substantially better.

It is easy to understand the attractiveness of a prorated $40,000 a year income against the average earnings of other workers in Canada when the average income for women of all ages was $9,522 in 1981 (*Women in the Labour Force*, 1984). The risks of harassment, arrest, and violence are fewer in the more protected work environment of a body parlor or up-market hotel although there are few real benefit arrangements. Where there are employment arrangements, employees often rely on customer tips rather than salaries (Prus & Stylliances, 1980). Badgley's (1984) analysis of the reasons for turning to prostitution is instructive:

> The reason given by most of the youths for turning to prostitution was that it afforded them the opportunity for *rapid financial gain* [emphasis added]: 66 boys (78.6%) and 95 girls (65.5%) said this was among their primary reasons for becoming prostitutes (p.991).

A smaller but significant portion of boys (29.8%) and girls (17.2%) reported inability to find employment as a primary reason for becoming prostitutes. Only a small percentage (11.4%) reported being forced or coerced into prostitution, although subtle and less dramatic inducements no doubt operate on these young people. What might be inferred from Badgley's survey of 229 male and female juvenile prostitutes regarding inducement to prostitution is this: while inability to find work remained the second most often reported inducement, opportunity for big fast money stood up as the single largest motivator. In Canada where youth unemployment is likely to hover close to 20% for the next few years, lack of work and marketable skills do appear to make prostitution a troubling but lucrative job creation strategy for a minority of young people. Although not studied explicitly, one conjectures that numbers of these young hookers were ignorant of access to social assistance, ineligible for assistance because of their transient lifestyle, and many were simply not prepared to subsist on welfare level incomes or low skill jobs. This type of young hooker is similar to the third class of prostitutes described in "The Social Evil":

> A third class, one which is more or less typical of American prostitution, is made up of those who cannot be said to be driven into prostitution either by absolute want or by exceptionally pernicious surroundings. They may be employed at living wages, but the prospect of continuing from year-to-year with no change from tedious and irksome labor creates discontent and eventual rebellion (cited in *Prostitution in America*, p.10).

Employment, job creation and retraining are rarely mentioned as treatment alternatives, although the Badgley Report (1984) does recommend circumscribed specialty programs:

> . . . the Government of Canada establish support for special multidisciplinary demonstration programs (child protection, police, education, medical and youth job training services) for five years (renewable) designed to reach and serve the needs of these youths, focusing upon: affording immediate protection; counselling; and education and job training (p.1047).

This recommendation is laudable in its acknowledgement of the training and employment problem. It brings to mind a passage by Freud written in 1907 acknowledging the not unrelated problem of sex education. Freud (1981) stated, "Hence, once again, we see the unwisdom of sewing a single silk patch onto a tattered coat—the impossibility of carrying out an isolated reform without altering the foundations of the whole system" (p.181).

The tattered coat in this instance is Canada's economic decline coupled with the more invidious ethic promising rapid financial gain. This need for rapid financial gain is a curious feature of the body politic. The subsistence needs of the body can usually be met through the subsistence level income of the welfare system, but in our economy it is hard to distinguish the subsistence needs of bodies from the insatiable need for social prestige associated with certain forms of consumption (O'Neill, 1985). The bodies of young hook-

ers, low on the total scale of social prestige, are inscribed with a
certain text vis-à-vis their need for prestige items from the cata-
logues of consumer culture. Young hookers, for example, enjoy
fast cars, expensive stereos, and more symbolically, expensive
drugs like cocaine, which put them in a league with sexualized
high-rollers like John DeLorean. The integration of sex into industry, commerce, and advertising has served to sexualize those certain
prestige products of Hugh Hefner's "Playboy" such as sports cars,
cocaine, liquor, and hi-tech toys, while simultaneously commo-
ditizing and objectifying women's bodies in the illusion of freedom
to pursue the good life.

This prescription of consumption channels for the expression of
libidinous energy in directions which are politically useful is fully
developed in the successive works of Marcuse (1955, 1964; Ober,
1982). This identification of sex and industry Marcuse develops
under the discussion of repressive or institutionalized desublima-
tion. This term refers to the repression and channeling of sexuality
through prescribed pathways of commerce and industry, while isolating the tender and erotic components which Freud posits as the
basis for all civilized human relationships. In this way, the bounda-
ries of sexual freedom appear to increase simultaneously with
greater control of the individual as consumer of sexualized commodities. For Marcuse, the Victorian morality of *The Contagious
Diseases Act* era has essentially the same status as the free market
shibboleth of today. Both are mythological in the sense that they
both illustrate great discrepancies between what is promised as the
model moral and economic fibre of the community and what is
practiced from day-to-day. The myth of unhampered free market
competition promoted in the Reaganomic discourse of 1984 prom-
ises a moral and equitable community but delivers something quite
different.

The *Playboy* and *Penthouse* agenda ghettoize into silence everything that does not fit with the freedom to pursue the good life:

> The paradox of modern corporate culture is that it panders
> to the libidinal body, titillating and ravishing its sensibilities,
> while at the same time it standardizes and packages libidinal
> responses to its products. In North America the libidinal body

politic is the creature of the corporate culture and its celebration of the young, white, handsome, heterosexual world of healthy affluence. In this sense the libidinal body is an unhealthy distortion of the political life of the community since it fails to cope with the poor, the sick, the aged, the ugly, and the black. Everything that fails to conform to its image of suburbinanity has to be segregated and pushed into the ghettos of race, poverty, crime, and insanity (O'Neill, 1985, p.140).

To use Foucault's (1978) terms, the same strategy commercializes sex, promotes scientific and quasiscientific studies of sexual performance, down to the measurement of genitalia and the selection of a spectrum of sexual accoutrements to improve performance. The same strategy gives us the celebration of Brooke Shields and Michael Jackson as pubescent sex icons in the sale of jeans, cosmetics, soft drinks and all manner of commercial claptrap. These sexualized, commoditized ego-ideals are standards forever beyond the means of ordinary people, frustrating them in their quest for the competitive youthful good life, and leaving them passively resigned and susceptible to whatever is offered instead. The sexual freedom arising from the sexual revolution of recent decades is the freedom to consume what is sexualized and the freedom to organize our deeroticized sexual interests around the corporate agenda.

The prospects for an overhaul of advertising regulations affecting the apparent age of models, or regulating erotic tenderness back into the imagery of human sexuality seem unlikely. Likewise, the overall shortage of jobs and decent wages for young people do not seem to be a much discussed intervention route in the current prostitution debate. In some respects it's surprising that more juveniles are not prostituting. Presumably, however, there is no free prostitution market anymore than with any other commodity. The ghettoized urban zones where young prostitutes circulate are well defended pieces of territory where only a certain number of bodies can circulate. A whole contraband economy operates there, controlling who cruises where and who works for and with whom. Moreover, what is requested by tricks in exchange for money runs from relatively vulnerable humane acts (tender clinging, conversations about loneliness and isolation) to brutalizing, violent acts against prostitutes which are strong disincentives to hook. The social exchange dimensions of juvenile prostitution are severely restricted. The wish to rise socially, characterized by symbolic consumption of prestige commodities, is frustrated through the ostracization of prostitutes from the social and family lives of their clients. Prostitution is a socially isolating and dangerous job, one with high pay, few benefits, and occupational risks, but one that nevertheless is a significant point of entry into the labor force for some young workers.

PROFESSIONAL REGULATION OF THE FAMILY

Much of the current concern over protecting children from prostitution arose as a consequence of increased public concern regarding sexual abuse. Since child abuse arose in the 1960s as an object of public concern, sexual abuse, runaways, and now juvenile prostitution have been successively constructed as objects of public concern (Weisberg, 1985). Streetproofing children is part of the contemporary scene. In practice, the protection of children is guided by what is in the "best interests" of the child. What is in the "best interests" of children, what legal and service remedies are available to them, what principles of family autonomy and children's rights should be considered? These are still hotly contested in decisions to terminate parental rights or bring children into care (Kintzer, 1984). The moral imperative of protecting children from harm has to be separated from assumptions that state intervention is *de facto* beneficial. The principle of the "least restrictive alternative" is increasingly considered as the least destructive and most demonstrably beneficial intervention. As Rutter (1984) reminds us, neither having the right intention nor proceeding with humane forms of intervention, grant immunity from harm. For example, with the best of intentions the educational and child welfare authorities in Canada have done considerable harm to Indian communities (Sullivan, 1983).

In the past two decades child welfare authorities, after a pattern of somewhat zealous placement of children in alternate care facilities, have come to the conclusion that the "best interests" of the child are generally served through the best interests of the family and placements have been declining. This is in part through the slow recognition that public caretaking is an enormously expensive undertaking with some questionable benefits. The depth and range of intervention suggested by reform related to sexual abuse and prostitution in the Badgley Report (1984), for example, need to be carefully weighed against the known benefits that will accrue.

There are no good data indicating an increase in sexual abuse, although reporting is certainly increasing since there is a greater awareness and a legal obligation to report. Vern Bullough (cited in Davis, 1982) argues that sexual abuse examined from almost any perspective is down radically from the immediate and remote past. It is down, he argues, because the factors affecting it most, family size, rural isolation, lack of awareness and legal penalties, are all more favorable now than ever before. What sectors promote unsubstantiated fears and ideas that sexual abuse is increasing?

Bledstein (1976) and McKnight (1985) have documented how professionals monopolize service production. There is a constant play on public fears of disorder and disease, embedded in deliberately mystifying jargon. Vernacular or home-spun remedies to social problems are diminished in credibility and an intensified demand for professional service is created. Deficiencies and disturbances are created that translate into the professional classes adopting, on behalf of the state, the socialization functions of the family. McKnight (1985) reminds us that a commodity intensive society such as we live in institutionally corrupts care. The need for care, that need for the self-conscious help on which the modern family is built, is the foundation of what Illich (1983) calls the "disabling professions." As an example, in referring to the need for expanded hospital-based treatment programs for sexual abuse, the Badgley Report (1984) states ". . . the efficacy of particular measures in improving the care and protection of these patients is unknown" (p. 669). Many of the benefits of intervention seem to do with improved or more rapid detection, investigation, professional collaboration, and counselling, in short, with the production needs of the service providers rather than direct benefits to the victim. These services were developed for the victim's benefit but at the present time their efficacy is at least dubious.

The need for services to the sexually abused child and family was not always evident. In fact, sexual abuse, that best kept secret, was not a topic to be taken seriously in Victorian times, if we can judge by Freud's colleagues. Freud presented his early version of the seduction theory in 1896 and got a very icy reception from his colleagues. Recently, however, Jeffery Masson (1984) rose to brief celebrity status by alleging Freud's cover-up about the prevalence and trauma of incestuous seductions. This high minded scandal unfolded in the pages of the *Times, New Yorker, Atlantic* and elsewhere. Masson argued that the Freudian seduction theory was abandoned by Freud in a long circuitous rationale to cover-up and protect Freud's colleague and confidant, Fleiss. The seduction theory essentially purported that sexual abuse (missbrauch) in early childhood was the cause of adult hysteria. This view Freud later retracted in his theoretical development of childhood sexuality and the Oedipus complex. The existence of widespread sexual contact between parents, or those in a position of trust, and children, now popularly called sexual abuse, was dismissed in Freud's time by Kraft-Ebbing as a "scientific fairy tale" (Masson, 1984, p.35). What was once bad for business is now good for business.

With increased contemporary focus on sexual abuse, there is a proliferation of manuals detailing standardized investigation/assessment protocols for investigating sexual abuse, as well as a host of treatment remedies for the victim, the offender, and the other family members (Lawton-Speert & Wachtel, 1983). There is much talk of incest survivors despite the lack of any cool-headed analysis of the short-term consequences, or prospective studies on the long-term consequences of incest. There is a great demand for sex abuse expertise. Constantine and Martinson (1981) observe that this is a conflicting and changing period relative to childhood sexuality. Fifty years ago Freud preached the ubiquity of the incestuous family romance. Today mere parental acknowledgment of incestuous feelings is considered abnormal and any research that distinguishes positive and negative incest experiences is seen as reprehensible, part of a campaign of the pro-incest lobby. In one of the few balanced reviews of 30 studies on the effects of child/adult sexual encounters, Constantine and Martin (1981) detail the effects of cross-generational sexual encounters from positive to neutral to extremely negative.

The question of whether or not sexual abuse and prostitution are linked in any simple way appears to be unclear. Myers (1980) talks about prostitution and self-mutilating behavior as survival skills in coping with the consequences of sexual abuse. James and Meyerding (1978) and Weisberg's (1985) sample of clinical populations show much higher than expected reports of sexual abuse. However, these are both distorted samples. Clinical samples are more likely to show sexual and physical abuse histories as well as greater familial discord, crowded and poor housing, and a number of other economic predictors of psychosocial risk described by Garmezy and Rutter (1984). Badgley's (1984) study of 229 unselected juvenile prostitutes surveyed on the street show no higher incidence of sexual abuse than other youth. Silbert and Pines (1981) surveyed 200 somewhat older youth on the street in order to avoid sampling of "service oriented" prostitutes like those picked up in the Weisberg (1985) study. Although lacking comparison data, Silbert and Pines (1981) show roughly 60% of their street sample as having histories of sexual abuse.

That victims of sexual abuse need treatment is more or less already accepted by helping professionals. There are some writers who have attempted to moderate claims regarding how injurious or disturbing incestuous experiences are (Bourgeois, 1979; Lukianowicz, 1972; Fox, 1980). Constantine and Martinson (1980) have differentiated the disturbing effects as a function of age and consent. If there existed a simple predictive relationship between incest/sexual abuse, and prostitution, prostitution would appear to have a familial cause, and aggressive family-based intervention would be warranted. In short, a clear link between abuse and prostitution would move the intervention level away from broader economic and social factors predicted by political choices and policies and creates a clear mandate and increased demand for the specialized helping professionals who make their incomes by constructing social problems and then setting out to remedy them.

Foucault (1978, 1979, 1980) pioneered historical research on the process whereby the subject of the modern welfare state is constituted through the professional discourse about sexed and familied bodies. Foucault identifies four independent lines along which specific mechanisms of knowledge and power historically become centered on sex. These are identified as (1) the hysterization of women's bodies; (2) the sexualization of children; (3) the socialization of procreative behavior; and (4) the psychiatrization of perverse pleasure. The family of today, according to Foucault (1978):

> . . . must not be understood as a social, economic, or political structure of alliance that excludes or at least restrains sexuality . . . on the contrary; its role is to anchor sexuality . . . the family is the interchange of sexuality and alliance; it conveys the law and the juridical dimension in the deployment of sexuality; and it conveys the economy of pleasure and the intensity of sensations in the regime of alliance (p.108).

> . . . then a pressing demand emanated from the family: a plea for help in reconciling these unfortunate conflicts between sexuality and alliance; and caught in the grip of this deployment of sexuality which had invested it from without, contributing to its solidification into its modern form, the family broadcast the long complaint of its sexual suffering to doctors, educators, psychiatrists, priests and pastors, to all the "experts" who would listen . . . The family was the crystal in the deployment of sexuality: it seemed to be the source of a sexuality which it actually only reflected and diffracted. By value of its permeability, and through the process of reflections to the outside, it became one of the most valuable tactical components of the deployment (p.111).

The family of former years has been gradually and strategically defamilized to the extent that individual rights are given prominence over family integrity. The second dimension of this strategy becomes the legal mandating of family centered interventions by what Donzelot (1979) calls the "tutelary complex" which is comprised of professional agencies who have taken on much of the authority and socializing function of the family in exchange for a clean bill of family health. A century ago the family fulfilled a number of social functions including economic, productive, educational, recreational, medical, and affectional. Today, the first five have been taken over by social institutions mediated by the church, state, and the tutelary complex. The affectional/erotic dimension of family life is under heavy scrutiny.

O'Neill (1983) argues that much of the current concern over the child's rights in the family parallels earlier Victorian concern about the child in the factory sweatshops, only now the factory is in the home! His analysis involves a skillful dissection of the intrusion of the liberal welfare state into domestic life. He develops his argument around a critique of feminist economics.

The ideology of feminist economics proposes a free economy of legal, contractual arrangements in lieu of the traditional family economy which it portrays as a slave economy. Without wishing to misrepresent radical feminist positions, one can safely credit feminists with a focussing of the family economy on individual rights backed up by legal reassurances. The logical development of this perspective reduces the family to an aggregate of neutered, ageless, interchangeable members, bound together by contracts: an isocracy.

These contracts define a contractual set of familial obligations in which men subcontract the work of family life to women and children. The inference here is that working men are the exploiters of their wives and children. Thus, families need the careful articulations of women's rights and children's rights to protect against the phallocracy of the father. This phallocracy also becomes responsible for prostitution:

> We do not see any difference between street walkers and call girls, or young male or female prostitutes. The customers are men, and men of all backgrounds. The problem is not prostitution, it's the phallocratic society itself which produces and sells prostitution by the power of male desire, and which ensures the organization and permanence of this sex market (Payeur, 1983, p.8, Authors Translation).

This embedding of the free market requirement of independently contracted legal agents into the definition of families debases what Illich (1983) calls "vernacular gender" into "economic sex" and simplifies or ignores our fragile familial interdependencies. Above all, this embedding promotes the myth of the neutered, ageless individual moving towards greater equality before the law. This caricature of the market model of the family is a predictable development in the radical monopoly of goods and services over human, familied need. It is partly against this backdrop that current enthusiasm over children's rights must be viewed. As we move towards the postindustrial era, characterized by an information and service economy, one would expect to see domestic life increasingly organized in accordance with the service products of the helping industry.

The discussion of defamilized rights is meant to heighten our sensitivity to liberal child protection legislation developed in the confines of growth-oriented economic systems. How children's rights are articulated in law will be affected by a number of power configurations and will be a blueprint of the family's indenturing on the broader economic fabric.

What is at stake in legislation controlling juvenile prostitution and sexual abuse is not simply a matter of protecting children. Nor is it simply an increasing articulation of the sexual rights of children. The sexual rights of children are not restricted to legislating the capacity to say no to adults or to the promotion of educational programs to define good and bad touching.

In the absence of enabling rights, advocacy for protection of the "unwilling or inappropriate audience" reduces to denial of minority rights. A modest version of these enabling rights might include the right to know about sexuality; the right to be sexual; the right to access to sexual materials, including contraceptives; the right to produce and distribute these materials; the right to affectional/erotic intimacy and so on (Calderone, 1977). A more radical version of these enabling rights bring us into the marginal liberation ideologies promoted by the Sexual Freedom League, Rene Guyon Society, North American Man Boy Love Association, and Pedophile advocacy groups (O'Carroll, 1980; Constantine & Martinson, 1981). These Pedophile groups strike a horrified chord in the hearts of many child protection advocates and make strange bedfellows with the children's rights lobby.

Any measures intended to promote the position and well being of children as sexual actors must address questions raised in the preceding pages: (1) which groups or classes define the "regime of truth" regulating juvenile and family sexuality and whose interests are served by this definition; (2) to what extent are sexually protective measures matched by enabling measures intended to reduce age discrimination and acknowledge the sexual expression of children and youth; and (3) to what extent does family life become isomorphic with the economy of the liberal welfare state and thus a mute structure of political and ideological reproduction?

REFERENCES

Bledstein, B.S. (1976). *The culture of professionalism*. New York: Norton.
Bourgeois, M. (1979). Comportements incestueux et psychopathologie. *Annales Medico-Psychologigues, 137*, 1008-1017.
Calderone, M.S. (1977). Sexual rights. *SIECUS REPORT, 5*,3.
Canadian Advisory Council on the Status of Women (C.A.C.S.W.) (1984). *Prostitution in Canada*. Ottawa: C.A.C.S.W.
Constantine, L. & Martinson, F. (1981). *Children and sex*. Boston: Little, Brown.
Davis, C. (1982). *Challenges in sexual science*. Iowa: Graphic Publishing.
Donzelot, J. (1979). *The policing of families*. New York: Random House.
Foucault, M. (1978). *The history of sexuality*. New York: Vintage Books.
Foucault, M. (1979). *Discipline and punish*. New York: Vintage Books.
Foucault, M. (1980). *Power/knowledge*. Toronto: Random House.
Fox, R. (1980). *The red lamp of incest*. Toronto: Clarke Irwin.
Freud, S. (1981). *On sexuality* (Vol. 1). Markham: Penguin Books.
Garmezy, N. & Rutter, M. (Eds.). (1983). *Stress, coping and development in childhood*. Toronto: McGraw-Hill.
Henriques, F. (1968). *Prostitution and society* (Vols 1-3). London: MacGibbon and Kee.
Hutt vs. The Queen (1978), 38 C.C.C. (2d) 418, 82 D.L.R. (3d) 95, 1 C.R. (3d) 164,[1978] 2 W.W.R. 247, 19 N.R. 331 (S.C.C.).
Illich, I. (1983). *Gender*. London: Marion Boyars.
James, J. & Meyerding, J. (1978). Early sexual experience as a factor in prostitution. *Archives of Sexual Behaviour, 7*, 31-42.
Kintzer, J. (1984). Children's rights in the family and society: Dilemmas and realities. In S. Chess & A. Thomas (Eds.), *Annual progress in child psychiatry* (pp. 527-544). New York: Brunner/Mazel.
Lawton-Speert, S. & Wachtel, A. (1983). *Child sexual abuse and incest: An annotated bibliography*. Ottawa: National Clearing House on Family Violence.

Lukianowicz, N. (1972). Incest, paternal incest, and other types of incest. *British Journal of Psychiatry, 120*:301-313.

Marcuse, H. (1955). *Eros and civilization*. Boston: Beacon Press.

Marcuse, H. (1964). *One dimensional man*. Boston: Beacon Press.

McKnight, J.L. (1985). *The mask of love: Professional care in the service economy*. New York: Marion Boyars.

Masson, J. (1984, February). Freud and the seduction theory. *The Atlantic Monthly*, pp. 33-53.

Myers, B. (1980). Incest: If you think the word is ugly take a look at its effects. In *Sexual abuse of children: Selected readings*. Washington: National Committee on Child Abuse and Neglect.

Nield, K. (1973). *Prostitution in the Victorian Age: Debates on the issues from 19th century critical journals*. Westmead: Gregg International.

Ober, J.D. (1982). On sexuality and politics in the works of Herbert Marcuse. In A. Brake (Ed.), *Human sexual relations* (pp. 82-107). New York: Penguin Books.

O'Carroll, T. (1980). *Paedophilia: The radical case*. London: Reter Owen.

O'Neill, J. (1982). Defamilization and the feminization of law in early and late capitalism. *International Journal of Law and Psychiatry, 5*, 255-269.

O'Neill, J. (1985). *Five bodies*. Ithaca: Cornell University Press.

Payeur, G. (1983). La prostitution des mineurs/es et des minoursees: Symptome de la phallocratie (Juvenile prostitution: Symptom of the phallocracy). In *La prostitution des Mineurs/es: Probleme ou solution*. Annales Du Colloque Tenu Les 24/25 Novembre 1983 A La Maison Du Citoyen Hull (Depot Legal-Bibliotheque National Du Canada).

Prus, R. & Styllianos, I. (1980). *Hookers, Rounders and Desk Clerks*, Toronto.

Prostitution in American: Three investigations, 1902-1914 (1976). (Social Problems & Social Policy Series). New York: The Arno Press.

Report of the committee on sexual offences against children and youths (Vols. 1 & 2) (1984). (The Minister of Justice and Attorney General of Canada, The Minister of National Health and Welfare). Ottawa: Minister of Supply and Services Canada.

Report of the special committee on pornography and prostitution (Vols. 1&2) (1985). (Ministry of Justice and Attorney General). Ottawa: Minister of Supply and Services Canada.

Rush, F. (1980). *The best kept secret: Sexual abuse of children*. New Jersey: Prentice-Hall.

Rutter, M. (1984). Prevention of children's psychosocial disorders: Dilemmas and realities. In S. Chess & A. Thomas (Eds.), *Annual progress in child psychiatry* (pp. 271-295). New York: Brunner/Mazel.

Shorter, E. (1975). *The making of the modern family*. New York: Basic Books.

Silbert, M. & Pines, A. (1981). Child sexual abuse as an antecedent to prostitution. *Child Abuse and Neglect, 5*, 407-411.

Sullivan, T. (1983). Native children in treatment: Clinical, cultural and social issues. *Journal of Child Care, I*: 75-87.

Tourism and Prostitution (1979, November). *ISIS: International Bulletin, 13*, 4-6.

Weisberg, K. (1985). *Children of the night: A study of adolescent prostitution.* Toronto: Lexington.

Westendorp vs. The Queen (1983) 2 C.C.C. (3d) 330.

Women in the labour force (Part 2) (1984). Labour Canada: Publications Distribution Centre.

Young, A. (1978). *Juvenile prostitution: A federal strategy for combatting its causes and consequences.* U.S. Department of Health, Education and Welfare.

Adolescent Suicide:
An Overview

Cathie Stivers

Suicide ranks among the 10 leading causes of death in the U.S., and poses a great threat to adolescents in particular. The following is a brief review of the dimension of the problem, the theories of its causes, and the precipitating events and warning signs associated with suicide attempts.

PREVALENCE

Suicide has now become the second leading cause of death among adolescents. Accounting for approximately 5000 deaths a year in the 15 to 24 age group, it trails only automobile and other accidents (Doan & Peterson, 1984). "Suicide rates per 100,000 adolescents aged 15 to 24 rose from 8.8 in 1970 to 12.5 in 1980, 1981 and 1982; a slight decline to 11.7 occurred in 1983" (Monthly Vital Statistics, 1984). These statistics represent conservative estimates due to the fact that suicide is underreported, intentionally as well as unintentionally. Further projections for the year 2000, based on the 11-year trend from 1968 to 1978, predict a 15.5 per 100,000 rate in the 15 to 19 age group (up from 8.0 per 100,000) and a 36.3 per 100,000 rate in the 20 to 24 age group (up from 16.9 per 100,000) (Depression, 1980).

Cathie Stivers is Assistant Professor, Department of Health Education, Physical Education and Recreation, University of New Mexico, Albuquerque, NM.

DEMOGRAPHY

Age- , sex- , and race-specific rates reveal different patterns regarding suicide completions, attempts, and methods. "Adolescents make many more attempts per successful suicide than do adults. The ratio for adolescents has been estimated as high as 120:1 (more conservative estimates are 20:1) while the adult ratio is approximately 8:1" (Rosencrantz, 1978: 209). The ratio of females to males in attempted suicide is 3:1 in the general population; that ratio increases to 9:1 in the adolescent population (Lester & Lester, 1971). Although females surpass males in suicide attempts, the success rate among males is three times as high as that of females (McIntosh, 1985). Firearms and explosives are the most popular method of suicide among both sexes, but their use is higher among males. Hanging/strangulation is the second most popular among males, while poisoning by solid or liquid substances is second among females (Depression, 1980). Suicide rates among the white population continue to exceed those of persons among other racial groups, in nearly all age ranges, for males and females, in spite of an overall increase among rates for nonwhites (McIntosh, 1985). Specifically, "the rates for white men and women have risen less than 20%, while the increase for black men and women has nearly doubled. Even with this increase, white men still have twice the rate of suicide of black men, and white women have three times the suicide rate of black women" (Eddy & Alles, 1983).

Geographically, the Mountain and Pacific regions of the U.S. show the highest suicide rates among all age groups (17.4 and 16.7 per 100,000 respectively), while the lowest rates are found in the Middle Atlantic region (9.6 per 100,000) (Ibid.). International comparisons reveal that the U.S. overall suicide rate approximates the median among rates of other developed countries (Ibid.; Healthy People, 1976).

Time variations in suicide rates appear during months of the year, days of the week, and even hours of the day. Suicidal deaths increase in the fall and the spring, and Sundays and Mondays are the days in which suicidal acts most prominently occur (Frederick, 1977). With respect to the time of day in which suicides occur, teenagers most frequently tend to commit suicide between the hours of 3 p.m. and midnight, whereas adults tend to commit suicide between midnight and dawn (McNeely, 1977).

THEORIES OF CAUSATION

Traditional theories of suicide causes originate from Sigmund Freud and Emile Durkheim. Freud's psychodynamic theory describes the adolescent as having experienced loss of love, deprivation, and rejection in relation to important persons in his/her life. Feelings of anger and resentment develop, but these impulses toward the adolescent's love objects create a sense of guilt. According to Freud's theory, suicide results when the adolescent's need to assuage the guilt turns into self-destructive attitudes and behavior (McKenry, Tishler & Christman, 1980). Expanding on Freudian concepts, Karl Menninger (1938) says that suicide is a composite death wish of wanting to kill, wanting to be killed, and wanting to die (Hart, 1978). This wish "may be followed by a long list of self-directed aggressions. A boy killing himself after a quarrel with his father is killing the introjected father" (Ibid: 370).

While Freud's theory is founded on principles of human psychology, Durkheim explains his suicide causation in sociological terms. He categorizes suicide into four types, each reflecting the social conditions under which a person kills himself: egoistic, altruistic, anomic, and fatalistic. Egoistic and altruistic suicides are caused by extreme degrees of integration, a term used by Durkheim to describe one's relationship with other people or groups. A low integration level leads to egoistic suicide, when a person has lost commonality with a group to the extent that his life becomes meaningless; contrarily, a high integration level leads to altruistic suicide, when group solidarity becomes so strong that one's individuality is disregarded. Anomic and fatalistic suicide inhabit the extreme ends of a similar continuum, this one labeled regulation. Regulation is regarded as the degree of control that social factors or external environment have over one's life. Anomic suicide is a result of a diminished social regulation to the degree that the person is frustrated and exasperated due to feelings of aimlessness; contrarily, fatalistic suicide is a result of such tight social regulation that the person sees his future blocked and his emotions checked

(Durkheim, 1951). "Suicide in the United States is generally of egoistic or anomic type" (Hardt, 1979).

In accordance with this sociological theory, McAnarney identifies specific social forces and their relationship to adolescent suicide (Denhouter, 1981):

1. In societies where family ties are close, suicidal rates are low and conversely, where families are not close, suicidal rates are high;
2. In cultures where the majority of people subscribe to a formal religion, it is generally believed that successful suicides are low, and where there is no formal religion, successful suicides are high;
3. Groups in transition have higher rates of successful suicides than stable ones;
4. Suicide rates are higher in societies where achievement is a major priority and lower where there is less pressure to achieve;
5. In cultures where the expression of aggressive feelings is suppressed, successful suicide increases, and where aggression is openly communicated, rates are lower.

Recently, suicidologists seem to agree that the interrelationships among man's external and internal environments rule out the single-cause explanation. Denhouter (1981) describes biophysical, sociological, and psychological principles in his theory of suicide. Masaryk (1970) identifies suicide as a conditioned result affected by natural causes (terrestrial and cosmic) and by human ones (physical conditions of bodily organization, general social conditions, political conditions, economic conditions, and conditions of spiritual culture). Smith (1976) describes the social-psychological theory which "sees self-destruction as a result of high personal ambition, keen rivalry, and the discrepancy between opportunity and meager results with resulting disappointment, guilt, and depression"; and the socio-cultural theory which considers a person's life-style and adaptive capability.

Cognitive theorists give strong consideration of an additional element in adolescent suicide that is not found in adult suicide. Death is still a somewhat romanticized notion in the minds of adolescents, and quite often the youth does not perceive death as a final, but rather a reversible process. This notion is nurtured by cultural attitudes as well as different media forms. "In some suicide attempts this irrational thinking is reflected in the attempter's hope to join a lost loved one, to make an important figure love him or to represent, symbolically, a rebirth after death" (McKenry, Tishler & Christman, 1980: 130).

In his extensive review of the literature, McIntosh (1985) summarizes:

> Applying the strict use of the term "theory" sociological approaches have come closest to suggesting testable, specific postulates, axioms, etc. that portend to explain suicidal behavior (as usually measured by suicide rates). Psychological proposals are more properly "mini-theories" or specialized hypotheses which attempt to explain various components or single facets of suicidal behavior, but not the more general phenomenon. No single theory exists which encompasses and considers the variety of contributing factors to suicide. Present theoretical notions do however provide us with some insight into why people kill themselves.

PRECURSORS AND WARNING SIGNS

Precursors are those events or conditions which precede, but may or may not contribute to, a suicide attempt. A list of such events, recorded by the Mayo Adolescent Health Program, includes the rupture of an intense relationship with a peer; occurrence of an event which lowers self-esteem, like expulsion from school, failure to make a team, or not being invited to a party; family discord; and parental separation, divorce, or death of a parent (Contreras, 1981). Other conditions include unwanted pregnancy, abortion, excessive use of alcohol or drugs by self or significant other, lack of quality communication between parent and adolescent, poverty, consistently poor academic performance, presence of physical deformities, pressure to meet high expectations, frequent moving from one neighborhood to another, a suicide attempt by a parent or someone close, and uncertainty of the future (Smith, 1976; Stivers, 1981; Wagman, 1978).

Warning signs are those behavioral (verbal or nonverbal) cues which are exhibited or expressed by a potential suicide. Most common among these are a drastic change in the teen's personal appearance and/or behavior, particularly from good to bad; a dramatic drop in school work; a sudden change in patterns of drug or alcohol use; fatigue and apathy; decreased appetite; truancy; giving away prized possessions; and depression (Smith, 1976; Stivers, 1981; Goldberg, 1981).

Although depression is the leading sign or symptom of suicide, the single best predictor is the occurrence and seriousness of a previous attempt (Hodgman, 1985). The American Association of Suicidology reveals that 86% of those successful have attempted suicide before. Lester and Lester add that of any ten people who kill themselves, eight have given definite warnings of their intentions (Lester & Lester, 1971). Additionally, approximately two thirds of all those who attempt suicide do not really wish to die: one third of them are ambivalent about their wishes, and only 3 to 5% are actually determined to commit suicide (Wekstein, 1979).

DISCUSSION

In light of the factual information provided, several points deserve attention which present implications and challenges for further research:

1. By dividing the 15 to 24 year age group into two groups, 15 to 19 and 20 to 24, one will find distinct differences with respect to suicide rates and risk. "Rates for both groups have doubled over the past 15 years, but 20 to 24-year-olds are at far greater risk for suicide, with rates twice as high as those for 15 to 19-year-olds. Intrapsychic and environmental tasks confronting middle and late adolescents aged 15 to 19 are different from those faced by young adults of 20-24 years" (Holinger, 1978: 756). What factors, if any, distinguish a 15-year-old suicide attempt from an 18-year-old attempt? Or a 21-year-old attempt?

2. Family discord has been identified as a common precursor to

adolescent suicide, as well as separation and divorce. Comparison of traditional vs. nontraditional family structure may reveal significant differences in teenage suicide rates. Where limited studies have compared two-parent families with one-parent families, consider the inclusion of these family settings: adopted children; children reared by a homosexual couple; children reared by grandparents, other relatives, or sibling; and children reared by unwed parent or parents. Clarification of mutually exclusive groups would be difficult, as would data collection. But the ever-changing complexion of "family" demands the identification of such diversity.

3. Today's American teenager finds him-herself in an age of instant satisfaction, quick disposal and replacement; in a land of plenty. As each generation of parents strive to provide their children with more and better than they had themselves, the conditions for adolescent anomie are perfected. When wishes are granted and material things obtained instantly and easily, the child misses the opportunity to develop self-pride, worth, and responsibility. This permissiveness leads to aimlessness . . . or does it? While many would agree with this explanation, is there empirical evidence that this is really what occurs? If the abstractness of this theory could be analyzed and quantified, a new set of social forces may be identified as significant contributory factors in adolescent suicide.

REFERENCES

Contreras, P. (1981). *Compendium of resource materials in adolescent health.* Rockville, MD: DHHS Publication No. (HSA) 81-5246. January.

Denhouter, K. V. (1981). To silence one's self: A brief analysis of the literature on adolescent suicide. *Child Welfare*, January, *60*(1), 2-10.

Depression in the 80s: A significant symposium. (1980). Lederle Laboratory Symposium. Monograph published by Science & Medicine, New York.

Doan, M. & Peterson, S. (1984). As "cluster suicides" take toll of teenagers. *U.S. News & World Report*, November 12, pp. 49-50.

Durkheim, E. (1951). *Suicide.* Translated by J. A. Spaulding & G. Simpson. New York: Free Press.

Eddy, J. M. & Alles, W. F. (1983). *Death education.* St. Louis: C. V. Mosby.

Frederick, C. J. (1977). Current trends in suicidal behavior in the United States. *American Journal of Psychotherapy, 32*(2), April, 172-200.

Goldberg, E. L. (1981). Depression and suicide ideation in the young adult. *American Journal of Psychiatry*, January, *138*(1), 35-40.

Hardt, D. V. (1979). *Death: The final frontier*. Englewood Cliffs, NJ: Prentice-Hall, Inc.

Hart, N. A. (1978). How teachers can help suicidal adolescents. *Clearinghouse*, Vol. 51, April, pp. 369-373.

Healthy people: The surgeon general's report on health promotion and disease prevention. (1979). U.S. DHEW(PHS) Publication No. 79-55071.

Hodgman, D. H. (1985). Recent findings in adolescent depression and suicide. Summer. *Journal of Development and Behavioral Pediatrics*, in press.

Holinger, P. C. (1978). Adolescent suicide: An epidemiological study of recent trends. *American Journal of Psychiatry*, June, *135*(6), 754-756.

Lester, G. & Lester, D. (1971). *Suicide: The gamble with death*. Englewood Cliffs, NJ: Prentice-Hall.

Masaryk, T. G. (1970). *Suicide and the meaning of civilization*. Translated by N. B. Werst & R. B. Batson. Chicago: University of Chicago Press.

McIntosh, J. L. (1985). *Research on suicide: A bibliography*. Westport, CT: Greenwood Press.

McKenry, P. C., Tishler, C. L. & Christman, K. L. (1980). Adolescent suicide and the classroom teacher. *The Journal of School Health*, March, pp. 130-132.

McNeely, J. D., Shafii, M. & Schwab, J. J. (1977). The student suicide epidemic. *Today's Education*, Sept./Oct., pp. 71-73.

Menninger, K. A. (1938). *Man against himself*. New York: Harcourt, Brace & Co.

Monthly Vital Statistics Report 32. (1985). #13, September 21, 1984. Hyattsville, MD: National Center for Health Statistics. In Hodgman, C. H., Recent findings in adolescent depression and suicide. Summer. *Journal of Developmental and Behavioral Pediatrics*, in press.

Rosenkrantz, A. L. (1978). A note on adolescent suicide: Incidence, dynamics and some suggestions for treatment. *Adolescence, 50*(13), Summer, 209-214.

Smith, D. F. (1976). Adolescent suicide: A problem for teachers? *Phi Delta Kappan*, April, *57*, 539-542.

Stivers, C. (1981). Adolescent suicide: Implications for educators. Unpublished paper.

Wagman, S. P. (1978). Adolescent suicide: A review. *The Osteopathic Physician*, December, pp. 10-15, 52-53.

Wekstein, L. (1979). *Handbook of suicidology: Principles, problems, and practice*. New York: Brunner/Mazel.

The Impact of Mothers' Incarceration on the Family System: Research and Recommendations

Donna C. Hale

INTRODUCTION

Beginning in the late 1950s, family investigators (Jackson, 1957; Bateson, 1961; Satir, 1964; Jackson & Weakland, 1961) who studied familial interactions began describing the family as a "system." Their usage of the term "family process" reflects the systemic orientation to describe the totality of family interactions. However, Kantor and Lehr (1975, x) indicated that although the multiplicity of observation by family investigators suggest that this system is a complex network of many different parts, no conceptual framework has been suggested that successfully demonstrates precisely the way in which these parts interrelate.

The purpose of this paper is three-fold. The first objective is to describe how family investigators have discussed the family in terms of systems language, i.e., homeostasis, equilibrium, and morphogenesis. This introductory discussion serves as a backdrop for my second purpose: to illustrate that the criminal justice system; specifically, the correctional system, seriously effects the inmate's family system by separating the offender from his/her family. Since rehabilitation and reentry of the offender into the community is the ultimate goal of the correctional system, it should be obvious that the maintenance of the offender's family system is of vital concern. If reentry into the community is to be successful, the returning of-

Donna C. Hale is Assistant Professor of Criminal Justice, University of Baltimore, Baltimore, MD 21201.

fender must be reentering a society where he/she will be supported by a family system or network which will strengthen his/her rehabilitation and prevent him/her from becoming a recidivist.

Similarly, there has been little research on the effects of separation of the incarcerated mother from her children. This oversight is crucial; not only because of the successful rehabilitation of the mother, but the future adjustment of her children. What happens to children whose mothers are incarcerated? Does incarceration result in higher incidents of mental illness or delinquent behavior? The separation of mother from her children is the third component of this paper. The paper concludes with recommendations for policy changes to meet the needs of the imprisoned mother and her children.

In the following section a discussion of the family as a system is presented. This presentation reflects how different family investigators have approached the problem from varying perspectives, and have made significant contributions to our understanding of the family as a system.

SYSTEMS THEORY AND FAMILY AS SYSTEM

Buckley in his book *Sociology and Modern Systems Theory* developed a general framework for approaching the investigation of sociocultural phenomena from a systems perspective. His framework consists of three overlapping entities: the system, the system's components or constituent members, and the system's significant environment. Buckley defines a system as a complex of elements or components which are directly or indirectly related in a mutually causal network, "such that at least some of the components are related to some others in a more or less stable way at any one time" (1967, 41).

He uses the terms system organization, system structure, and interrelations of components interchangeably and synonymously to refer to the system's primary function of mediating between both internal and external changes, or pressures to change, and the operations or behavior of the system and its members. Buckley postulates that social systems must be capable of morphogenesis or of changing their basic structure, organization, and values in order to survive and remain viable. Applying Buckley's conception of systems, the family can be seen as a self-organizing system constantly changing and elaborating behaviors in response to selective aspects of the external environment and demands of its own members. The active agents choosing the internal and external factors they respond to however, are the family members themselves (Aldous, 1970, 254).

Riskin (1963, 343) views the family as an ongoing system tending to

> . . . maintain itself around some point of equilibrium which has been established as the family evolves. The system is a dynamic, not a static, one. There is a continuous process of input into the system, and thus a tendency for the system to be pushed away from the equilibrium point. . . . Over a period of time, the family develops certain repetitive, enduring techniques or patterns of interaction for maintaining its equilibrium when confronted by stress; this development tends to hold whether the stress is internal or external, acute or chronic, trivial or gross. These techniques, which are assumed to be characteristic for a given family, are regarded as homeostatic mechanisms.

Generally, the concept of family system implies that all parts of the family are in some way in mutual interaction. Consequently, the concept of system is familiar in research on families under stress.[1] However, Hansen and Hill offer several cautions regarding system theory as an adequate theory of families under stress (1964, 787):

1. The family may in most cases be described with system concepts, but it does not necessarily display the characteristics of a system. Reequilibration, in particular, is not essential in family life.

2. Current system theories are quite inadequate for even description of the full range of human life, for they emphasize orderly arrangement and stability, rather than creative activity.

3. System theory is limited in developing an adequate theory of family functioning. It offers at most a methodological theory that can aid only in describing families. Current tendencies in using the system analogue (and the analogues of "function" and "dysfunc-

tion"), however, smack of three real dangers: (a) the danger of reifying the concepts so that families are seen as actually striving for homeostasis; (b) the danger of assuming that any such tendencies to homeostasis causally bring about action; and (c) the neglect of the full range of individual and family life and activity in stress situations.

Although the above three caveats submitted by Hansen and Hill negate the concept of system to family, systems theory has appeal to family research primarily for two reasons: (1) its focus on the activity of groups (family can be classified as a group); and (2) since intrafamilial group interaction is often extremely complicated, systems theory permits generalization about this complexity.

Hill (1971 in Stolte-Heiskanen, 1974, 594) states that general systems theory is relevant to the study of the family, since the family may be viewed as a "relatively closed (or open) system: a purposive, goal-oriented, task performing system that maintains a morphogenic equilibrium with its environment." Stolte-Heiskanen (Ibid.) explains that Hill's definition implies that in the process of interaction and survival, the family as a system responds to change by changing its structure.

The definition that Hill gives the family as a system is of particular importance for the examination of the incarcerated mother and her children. First of all, the children may adapt to the mother's incarceration by fabricating stories of where the mother is; secondly, the structure of the family changes depending on who assumes caretaking responsibility for the children, i.e., family members or foster parents.

To conclude, it must be reiterated that an important reason for the study of the family as a system is the need for a typology that differentiates families in accordance with distinctively different whole-family processes. In addition, it is important to look at families in a systemic model in order to develop a model for researchers and therapists who work with families to explain what happens in families. As indicated by Kantor and Lehr, a model with a common vocabulary for discussing family-system events is necessary in order for "researchers, therapists, and their students of family to know with some certainty what the other is talking about" (1975, x).

THE IMPACT OF THE CRIMINAL JUSTICE SYSTEM ON THE FAMILY

Edmund Cahn (1962, 30) has argued that a study of the impact of the criminal justice system on the family is necessary, since it is impractical to attempt an understanding of our laws and institutions without examining the impact of those laws and institutions on the lives and experiences of human beings they affect. He said, "It is these personal impacts that constitutes the criteria for an appraisal we may make."

Studies (Bakker et al., 1978; Bonfanti et al., 1974; DuBose, 1975; McGowan & Blumenthal, 1976; Zalba, 1964) have been conducted describing the impact that the criminal justice system has on family relationships. Justifiably, most of these studies focus on the correctional stage, since it is at this stage that the homeostasis of the family is affected. Pauline Morris in a 1965 study examined the practical problems encountered by inmates' families in their everyday lives: stigmatization, finances and housing, loneliness, management of children, and visits with the inmate. She concluded that, "the families of prisoners suffer disabilities which stem from situations which they themselves have not, for the most part, brought about. Every stress suffered by such families weakens the family and increases the likelihood of other family members, especially the children, becoming social casualties (1965, 11). She made the following recommendations: that there was a need for (1) financial provisions for prisoner's families; (2) improvement of social casework in prisons; and (3) improvement of facilities for contact between the prisoner and his/her family (Ibid., 14). Cavan and Zemans stressed the need for rehabilitating the family prior to the release of the prisoner (1958, 139). In another study, James Blackwell examined the effect of forced separation due to imprisonment on the family. He found that the adjustment of the family to enforced separation is a function of the marital adjustment existing between spouses prior to the separation. Blackwell inferred that the adjustment of the family to the separation is directly related to the wife's perception of the imprisonment situation as a crisis (1959, 22).

Blackwell concluded that imprisonment is different from other forms of family separation because there appears to be a demoralization connected with imprisonment which is not to be found in other forms of involuntary separation other than, perhaps, desertion. Imprisonment carries with it a stigma that is difficult for families to eradicate, especially if children are involved in the family relationship and structure (Ibid.). Children often have reported that they did not want anyone to think that their parent was a criminal; consequently, they did not tell anyone, except perhaps for a best friend that the child trusted not to tell anyone else.

It is evident from studies conducted that the major problems encountered by inmates' families are related to stigmatization, finances and housing, loneliness, management of the children, and visits with the inmate. However, these needs of the family are not considered. To date, the intactness of and the role of the family system has largely been ignored.

However, research has been conducted that indicates a strong positive relationship between the maintenance of strong family ties during imprisonment and the success of parole after an inmate has been released. Holt and Miller (1972, 61) found that only 50% of their group with no visitors during imprisonment were arrest-free during their first year of parole; for those with three or more visitors, the arrest-free rate for the same period was 70%. They also found that the men in the group with no visitors were six times more likely to be returned to prison during the first year than were the men in the group with three or more visitors (12% returned vs. 2% returned). Citing similar results found in Illinois and various other locations, Holt and Miller concluded that:

> . . . the positive relationship between strength of social ties and success on parole has held up for 45 years of release across very diverse offender populations in different localities.

Another study by Glaser (1964, 379) indicated that the fewest parole failures are men who when released live with their wives, whereas the greatest number of parole failures are men who when released live alone. He concludes that "marriages that can survive the husband's imprisonment seem clearly to be a major asset." However, marriage seems to be the relationship most vulnerable to deterioration during imprisonment. Holt and Miller (1974) discovered that 25% fewer wives of first-term prisoners were still visiting after three years.

It is evident from the literature that incarceration presents a crisis for the family. From the time an individual is accused to the period following release from prison and his/her community reintegration, the whole family goes through numerous stages of stress. Incarceration puts heavy burdens on family members in terms of role changes; the loss of a parent, child rearing difficulties and continual financial deprivation (Bain, 1978).

In the next section, the impact that imprisonment has on incarcerated women and their children is presented. This discussion indicates that although it has been acknowledged that imprisonment has an impact on the incarcerated male's relationship with his family, few studies have been conducted pertaining to how incarceration effects women and their children.

DISRUPTION OF HOMEOSTASIS: INCARCERATED MOTHERS AND THEIR CHILDREN

The incarceration of mothers is of particular concern to family system research for several reasons. One of the major dilemmas of a mother's incarceration is the care of her children during the time she is confined. (In the case of father institutionalization, his children are often cared for by his wife or by the grandparents; consequently, he does not experience the stress that the incarcerated mother does.) Not only is there stress for the confined mother, but her children as well. McGowan and Blumenthal (1976, 128) stated that "inmate mothers suffer a great deal of uncertainty and anguish. They often feel that enforced separation from their children is one of the most difficult aspects of their incarceration." Cottle (1976) reported that the incarceration of the mother may be very detrimental to her children and that the incarceration of a parent may decrease the self-esteem of children and increase their feelings of abandonment and loneliness.

One reason cited for the scarcity of research on the inmate mother and her children is the uncertainty surrounding the actual number of children that incarcerated women have (McGowan & Blumenthal,

1976, 121). In a recent study by Baunach (1985, 25) of two women's prisons in Kentucky and Washington State, she found that "the mothers interviewed had a total of 300 children or an average of 2.2 children each. About 84% of the mothers had 3 children or less." McGowan and Blumenthal (Ibid.) indicate a second reason for the meager information on the incarcerated mother and her children is the focus on the rights of the individual not the family unit; and the third reason is the lack of a national family policy, i.e., no effort is made to evaluate policies and practices in the criminal justice system in terms of their impact on family life. As McGowan and Blumenthal point out (1976, 121):

> Every component of the correctional system is oriented toward the punishment — and perhaps rehabilitation of the offender. Success is measured in terms of recidivism rates, not in terms of the degree to which offenders can be reintegrated into society or in terms of the impact of their experiences in the correctional system on their families or communities. The idea that the criminal justice system should take any responsibility for what happens to children of offenders is totally alien to the traditional concept of police, the judiciary or corrections.

These writers conclude that "at present, almost nothing is being done for inmate mothers and their children." This statement was written in 1976 and, unfortunately, little has changed in the criminal justice system (arrest, pretrial, detention, sentencing, and imprisonment) policies in the past decade.

Several policy recommendations have been proposed for the treatment of this population, and I believe these recommendations still merit recognition by the criminal justice system. First, there must be some consideration of the child's welfare at each point in the criminal justice system. For example, training police officers to recognize and consider needs of dependent children at the time the mother is arrested; attorneys should consider the child's needs when preparing the mother's case; pretrial investigation and presentence investigation reports should include specific mention of the defendant's family responsibility and this factor should be considered when recommendations are made to the court. Judges should consider the needs of children when making decisions about pretrial release, bail, and sentencing. At the correctional level, the staff should be trained to adopt a family-centered approach to inmates, and parole boards should be encouraged to consider a woman's family responsibility and needs of her children when making decisions about parole. Finally, the criminal justice and social service systems must develop closer policy coordination and service integration "if women prisoners and their children are to be treated more appropriately. This requires the development of linkages between these two systems and allocation of responsibility for the provision of needed services at every point in the criminal justice system" (McGowan & Blumenthal, 1976, 132-134).

Baunach (1985, 8) believes that the development of intervention programs designed to maintain continuing contact between inmate mothers and their children during her incarceration is important.[2] These interventions include nursery care within the prison or maintenance of family in small units in the community under close supervision; developing programs designed to prepare inmate mothers for coping realistically with their roles as mothers following release; and providing furloughs for inmate mothers, free transportation for their families to the prison and conjugal visits to maintain family cohesiveness. Finally, in order to maintain greater sensitivity to a family-oriented approach regarding inmate mothers, a variety of programs designed to improve mother-child relationships should be developed within the institution. Program suggestions include open and extended visiting, family counseling, child care courses, or "mother release" programs.

While the above is a composite of recommendations from earlier studies, I would also recommend that more evaluation research be conducted to ascertain the effect that programs such as Aid to Incarcerated Mothers (AIM) and Mother Offspring Life Development (MOLD) are having not only on recidivism rates of mothers, but the impact that these programs have on the self-esteem and well being of the children. In addition, it would be beneficial to examine the impact that these programs have on the caretakers of the children during the time the mothers are confined. Markeley (1972) has suggested that it would be important to observe how family ties are effected by rehabilitation programs during the period of incarceration and how they effect inmate adjustment following release, and whether or not family ties are strengthened.

Finally, it would be most interesting to see a replication of the Kinderheim program that was implemented in the mid-1970s by Helga Einsile in West Germany. It was her belief that if preschool children are allowed to remain with their incarcerated mothers, the children, mothers and ultimately the nation would benefit (Haley, 1980, 347-348).

NOTES

1. Burgess' study of families in depression, war reunion, and other stresses have emphasized the "readjustment" of families and the "equilibrating" of family troubles. See Hansen and Hill, "Families Under Stress," in Christensen, H.T. (ed.), *Handbook of Marriage and the Family*, Chicago: Rand McNally and Company, 1964, p. 787.

2. Baunach says that this problem is especially acute since between 50% and 70% of incarcerated women have one or more dependent children who were living with them prior to their imprisonment. Moreover, the average number of children for each inmate-mother is between two and three (from McGowan & Blumenthal, 1978; Zalba 1964; Bonfanti et al., 1974) and many of the incarcerated women have children younger than 13 (see note #1 of Baunach, 1985, p. 11).

REFERENCES

Aldous, J. (1970). "Strategies for Developing Family Theory." *Journal of Marriage and the Family*, 32 (November): 250-258.

Bahr, S.J. (1979). "Family Determinants and Effects of Deviance," in W.R. Burr, R. Hill, F.I. Nye & I.L. Reiss (eds.), *Contemporary Theories about the Family: Research-Based Theories*, Volume 1. New York: The Free Press.

Bain, Alastair (1978). "The Capacity of Families to Cope with Transitions: A Theoretical Essay." *Human Relations*, 31 (8): 675-688.

Bakker, L.J., B.A. Morris & L.M. Janus (1978). "Hidden Victims of Crime." *Social Work*, (March): 143-148.

Bateson, G. (1961). "The Biosocial Integration of Behavior in the Schizophrenic Family," in N.W. Ackerman, F.L. Beatman & S.N. Sherman (eds.), *Exploring the Base for Family Therapy*. New York: Family Service Association of America.

Baunach, P.J. (1985). *Mothers in Prison*. New Brunswick: Transaction Books.

Blackwell, J. (1959). *The Effects of Involuntary Separation on Selected Families of Men Committed to Prison from Spokane County, Washington*, Dissertation. State College Washington.

Bonfanti, M. et al. (1974). "Enactment and Perception of Maternal Role of Incarcerated Mothers." Masters thesis. Louisiana State University, May.

Broderick, C. & J. Smith (1979). "The General Systems Approach to the Family," in W.R. Burr, R. Hill, F.I. Nye & I.L. Reiss (eds.), *Contemporary Theories about the Family: General Theories/Theoretical Orientations*, Volume II. New York: The Free Press.

Buckley, W. (1967). *Sociology and Modern Systems Theory*. New York: Prentice-Hall.

Cahn, Edward (1962). *The Predicament of Democratic Man*. New York: Dell Publishing.

Cavan, R. & E. Zemans (1958). "Marital Relationships of Prisoners." *Journal of Criminal Law, Criminology and Police Science*, 49 (May-June).

Cottle, T.J. (1976). "Angela: A Child-Woman." *Social Problems*, 24: 516-523.

Currie, E. (1985). *Confronting Crime: An American Challenge*. New York: Pantheon Books.

DuBose, D. (1975). "Problems of Children Whose Mothers are Imprisoned." New York: Institute of Women's Wrongs. Mimeographed.

Glaser, D. (1964). *The Effectiveness of a Prison and Parole System*. Indianapolis, IN: Bobbs-Merrill Co.

Haley, J. (1962). "Family Experiments: A New Type of Experimentation." *Family Process*, 1: 265-293.

Haley, K. (1980). "Mothers behind Bars: A Look at the Parental Rights of Incarcerated Women," in S.K. Datesman & F.R. Scarpitti (eds.), *Women, Crime and Justice*. New York: Oxford University Press, Inc.

Hansen, D. & R. Hill (1964). "Families under Stress," in H.T. Christensen (ed.), *Handbook of Marriage and the Family*. Chicago: Rand McNally and Company.

Hill, R. (1949). *Families under Stress: Adjustment to the Crises of War Separation and Reunion*. New York: Harper and Brothers, Publishers.

Hill, R. (1971). "Modern Systems Theory and the Family: A Confrontation." *Social Sciences Information*, 10: 7-26.

Hirschi, T. (1983). "Crime and the Family," in J. Wilson (ed.), *Crime and Public Policy*. San Francisco: ICS Press, 53-68.

Holt, N. & D. Miller (1972). *Explorations in Inmate Family Relationships*. Sacramento, CA: Research Division, California Department of Corrections (January).

Jackson, D.D. (1957). "The Question of Family Homeostasis," *Psychiatric Quarterly*, (Supplement), 31: 79-90.

Jackson, D.D. & J.H. Weakland (1961). "Conjoint Family Therapy: Some Considerations on Theory, Technique, and Results." *Psychiatry*, (Supplement to Number 2) 24: 30-45.

Jackson, D.D. & E. Yalom (1965). "Conjoint Family Therapy as an Aid to Intensive Psychotherapy," in Benton, A. (ed.), *Modern Psychotherapeutic Practice*. Palo Alto: Science and Behavior Books.

Kantor, D. & W. Lehr (1975). *Inside the Family*. San Francisco: Jossey-Bass Publishers.

Lundberg, D., Sheckley, A. & Voelkar, T. (1975). "An Exploration of the Feelings and Attitudes of Women Separated from Their Children Due to Incarceration." Masters thesis. Portland State University.

McCubbin, H.I., C.B. Joy, A.E. Cauble, J.K. Comeau, J.M. Patterson & R.H. Needle (1980). "Family Stress and Coping: A Decade Review." *Journal of Marriage and the Family*, 42 (November): 855-871.

McGowan, B.G. & K.L. Blumenthal (1976). "Children of Women Prisoners: A Forgotten Minority," in L. Crites (ed.), *The Female Offender*. Lexington, MA: D.C. Heath and Company.

Markeley, C.W. (1973). "Furlough Programs and Conjugal Visiting in Adult Correctional Institutions." *Federal Probation*, 37 (March): 19-26.

Melville, J. (1976). "Society at Work: The Waiting Wives." *New Society*, 20 (May): 417-418.

Morris, P. (1965). *Prisoners and Their Families*. New York: Hart Publishing Company.

Riskin, J. (1963). "Methodology for Studying Family Interaction." *Archives of General Psychiatry*, 8: 343-348.

Satir, V. (1964). *Conjoint Family Therapy*. Palo Alto: Science and Behavior Books.

Skynner, A.C. Robin (1976). *Systems of Family and Marital Psychotherapy*. New York: Brunner/Mazel, Publishers.

Stolte-Heiskanen, V. (1974). "Social Indicators for Analysis of Family Needs Related to the Life Cycle." *Journal of Marriage and the Family*, (August): 592-600.

Wiseman, J.P. (1981). "The Family and Its Researchers in the Eighties: Retrenching, Renewing, and Revitalizing." *Journal of Marriage and the Family*, 43 (May): 263-265.

Wolfram, E. (1973). "Developing Values through Milieu Therapy," in B. Ross & C. Shireman (eds.), *Social Work Practice and Social Justice*. Washington, DC: National Association of Social Workers.

Zalba, S. (1964). *Women Prisoners and Their Families*. Sacramento: State of California Department of Social Welfare and Department of Corrections, (June).

Juvenile Justice and the Family: A Systems Approach to Family Assessment

Johnny E. Mc Gaha
David G. Fournier

INTRODUCTION

The juvenile court was founded around the turn of the century as a result of the movement to remove young offenders and wayward children from the harsh treatment inflicted in the adult criminal justice system. The new juvenile philosophy was based on the concept of "parens patriae" which places the state or court in the position of parent when it deems necessary, for the best interest of the child. This concept has been taken much too literally over the years resulting in the common practice of the court removing juvenile offenders from their families. The premise supporting this philosophy is that the state institution or facility can do a much better job of providing parental-like care than the parents.

Even when a young offender is placed on probation and allowed to remain in the home, the juvenile court caseworkers spend the majority of time working with the child rather than the family. According to Joseph Rowan (1976) former director of the Florida Juvenile System, 90% of the State's efforts are being focused on the individual and minimal attention is given to the family. Any attention the family receives usually occurs at the intake stage when a child is first referred, during some crisis or court hearing. In spite of

Johnny E. Mc Gaha is Assistant Professor, Criminal Justice Department, Southeast Missouri State University, Cape Girardeau, MO 63701. David G. Fournier is Associate Professor, Department of Family Relations and Child Development, Oklahoma State University, Stillwater, OK.

this lack of involvement with families by juvenile justice professionals, over 95% of the juveniles removed from their homes eventually return. Often to the same family or related problems that caused their problems to begin with. Any positive changes that the youth made while away are often negated in time as the youth returns to some type of acting-out behavior.

Institutional abuse of juveniles while in institutions have been widespread and well-documented in this country. Juveniles are often mistreated by agents of the state that are supposed to be protecting them. Juvenile experts have often labeled institutions as schools of crime (Pisciotto, 1982; James 1970; Wooden, 1977), as they make allegations that delinquents often turn into hard-core criminals while there. Institutions, by their very nature and even under the best of circumstances, hardly appear to provide the warm and supportive environment that the "parens patriae" philosophers had in mind. According to Rowan (1976), the "parens patriae" concept is wrong and should be replaced by a parental supporter movement that would focus on helping the family of the delinquent child.

FAMILIES AND DELINQUENCY: GENERAL RELATIONSHIPS

The review of the literature on the subject of families and delinquency strongly supports the role of the family in delinquent behavior. Researchers, for example, have found that youths who lack closeness with mothers and fathers are more likely to engage in delinquent acts. Robinson (1978), in studying the child rearing and disciplinary methods of parents of delinquents, found such parents were: inconsistent rule setters, less likely to praise, showed little genuine interest in their children, and demonstrated high levels of hostile detachment. Similarly, Richard Smith and James Walters (1978), found that factors which distinguished a sample of nondelinquents from a sample of incarcerated youths were associated with lack of a warm, loving, supportive relationship with the father, along with minimal paternal involvement, high maternal involvement and broken homes. Aichorn (1969), found that in all the families with a delinquent child, some type of conflict or disturbance was present in family relationships.

PARENTAL INFLUENCES AND ADULT CRIMINALITY

Goldstein (1974) concluded after extensive interviews with professionals who worked with violent offenders, that the agreed upon predictors of adult violent crime were parent centered including factors such as a childhood history of maternal deprivation, poor father identification, as well as abuse by one or more parent. In a 30 year follow-up study of 210 boys, McCord (1979) also found that negative parental influences were highly predictive of later serious criminal behavior. She found that 36% of the incidence of later violent criminality could be accounted for by childhood predictive factors. Boys who lacked supervision, whose mothers lacked self-confidence, or who had been exposed to parental conflict and to aggression, were likely to be convicted for serious personal crimes. Other studies (Glueck & Glueck, 1950; Farrington & West, 1975), have also documented strong correlations between parental influence and crime. Negative family influences are believed to contribute to the delinquent behavior of children chiefly because the family is the primary unit involved in teaching values and attitudes. Consequently, values and attitudes learned through the family govern the actions of the children throughout their lives.

In 1967, the President's Commission on Law Enforcement and Administration of Justice determined that the nation's juvenile justice system had not been successful in rehabilitating troubled youth or stemming the rising crime rates among juveniles. This task force also emphasized the importance of the family as a vital component of the delinquency problem. The commission recommended assistance be given to the family to enable it to function as a unit, rather than as a divergent collection of anonymous human beings. One of the major recommendations of the Commission was that counseling and therapy for the problem family be made easily available. In 1976, the National Advisory Commission on Criminal Justice Standards and Goals concluded in a report on juvenile justice and delinquency prevention that programs should be designed to insure that all children are raised in home situations beneficial to their growth. In spite of such strong recommendations by national commissions, true family-oriented programs in juvenile court programs are the exception rather than the rule. Traditional treatment approaches utilized by juvenile court agencies tend to follow the adult probation model which focuses on external controls through basic supervision, casework and monitoring. This approach, which provides opportunities for reinforcement of the juveniles good behavior and negative sanctions for bad, has often been criticized for its ineffectiveness (Presidents Commission, 1967).

When a juvenile's home environment is characterized by hostility, tension, stress, conflict and/or inadequate socioeconomic resources it's very difficult for him to internalize external threats or consequences. What he really needs is for someone to help the family learn better ways to relate to each other and to cope with their external problems. This is not to imply that the young offender should be relieved of his responsibility for his actions. Appropriate accountability is in itself therapeutic for juvenile offenders but it should be coupled, whenever practicable, with family-oriented assessment and intervention.

OUTCOME RESEARCH: JUVENILE COURT FAMILY PROGRAMS

There have been a number of studies that indicate strong support for family programs versus other types of counseling or casework. Johnson (1977) conducted a study which evaluated family counseling with repeat offenders under ongoing court supervision. He found that family counseling was significantly more effective than the traditional services such as routine probation casework. McPherson, McDonald and Ryer (1983) also found that family counseling was considerably more effective than probation services in reducing the number of recidivists, as well as the amount of recidivism. The statistical evidence from the above study suggest that family counseling has a strong impact on reducing the number of children under court supervision who repeat offenses. Similar studies have been reported in the Sacramento, California Juvenile Court (Baron, Feeny & Thornton, 1973), and in Florida (Whitt, 1979). Stringfield (1975) studied juveniles who had been part of a family counseling program in a residential treatment center and compared them to a control group receiving traditional peer group counseling in the same center. He found that those involved in family therapy also did significantly better in terms of recidivism at a one year follow-up, than those who were in the peer-oriented group. Studies by the National Resource Center on Family-Based Services indicate that intensive, family-based services, are a cost-effective alternative to removing children from troubled homes (Hutchison, 1982).

There is also very promising evidence that not only might the delinquent child benefit from family intervention but that it may have a deterrent effect on siblings from becoming delinquent. James Alexander and his associates (Klein, Alexander & Parsons, 1977) utilized family-oriented interventions with delinquent adolescents. Follow-up studies revealed that not only the delinquents behavior improved but the nontreated younger siblings of the targeted delinquent youth showed significantly less delinquent behavior, 3-1/2 years after treatment. His findings suggest that the family intervention may have had a true primary prevention effect.

FAMILY ASSESSMENT AND DIAGNOSIS

As stated previously, there has been a general reluctance on the part of juvenile court caseworkers to work with the entire family unit. Many feel that they are not qualified to do family intervention even though in many cases they are the only resource available to the family. A major hindrance for these workers has been the lack of a family-based diagnostic assessment procedure which would enable juvenile agencies to collect appropriate information for family system intervention. Even among family therapists there is a lack of consensus about the diagnostic process. A major problem with many diagnostic techniques currently in use is that they are not only individually biased, but symptom focused.

According to Olson (1980), the family systems behave differently than individuals and require different methods of diagnosis leading to selection of appropriate treatment strategies. Specific problems are relatively easy to identify but may have little real relation to the underlying family dysfunctions which may be contributing to the problem. Many problem families are encountering multiple symptoms and may be receiving treatment from several competing agencies, often without coordination. In multiproblem families it is not uncommon for as many as 6 to 10 different agencies and/or individuals to be involved with one family and working at cross purposes. The following actual case from the author's case files will help illustrate.

Susan, age 14, was referred to the juvenile office for truancy and incorrigibility. Her parents were having trouble controlling her at home and they "wanted something done with her." The juvenile court intake office had also received a referral from the school attendance officer on her younger brother, age 12, for truancy. During the intake interview it was learned that Susan had had an abortion earlier in the year and that her behavior at home and school had deteriorated since that time. The intake officer determined that Susan needed counseling and possibly temporary placement outside the home until the situation between parents and child improved. Susan was placed on informal supervision and referred to child welfare for possible crisis placement. She was also referred to the local mental health clinic where she was to begin weekly counseling sessions. The mental health center also determined that the mother was experiencing extreme emotional distress and she was placed with a counselor for regular therapy. The juvenile court intake officer later learned that Susan was seeing the school counselor for her school related problems and had been receiving counseling and birth control assistance since her abortion from the family planning service. Both Susan and her mother reported that the father drank excessively and that the parents had constant conflict.

Virtually every family member was experiencing symptoms in a different way. There were a total of five different agencies and at least six different individuals involved with the family, none of whom coordinated or communicated with each other in a systematic way. Some of the agencies had no knowledge of any of the others involvement with the girl and unfortunately, this situation is not unusual with welfare or juvenile court cases. The family, not surprisingly, continued to dysfunction until Susan was ultimately placed in a local girls' group home. She adjusted remarkably well almost immediately. The maximum stay at the program was six months and most girls returned home after their stay. One of the requirements of the treatment program was total family involvement in weekly sessions. The family attended regularly and the family system improved sufficiently to allow for Susan's successful return home. As this case illustrates the various individual efforts with individual family members appeared to be doing little good and was possibly making matters worse. It wasn't until one agency intervened appropriately with the entire family that the individual symptoms eased.

The need for systemic family assessment in the juvenile justice and welfare field is obvious. Approaches that focus on the adolescent's behavior as the problem are very limiting and narrow from a treatment perspective. Family-based therapies, particularly systems therapy, incorporates a broader theoretical perspective in assessing the adolescent's problem and provides for a much more comprehensive, effective approach.

THE CIRCUMPLEX MODEL

Olson and his colleagues (1979), proposed that instead of focusing upon presenting symptoms, emphasis should be placed on understanding the type of family system. There may not be any relationship between the presenting problem and the type of family system and treatment technique and treating the symptom without changing the family system will only provide temporary symptomatic relief.

Supporting this contention, Killorin and Olson (1984), reported on four consecutive families that came for treatment with the presenting symptom being an alcoholic family member. Even though each family member had the same presenting complaint, all four family systems were found to be very different. In traditional symptom-oriented programs, all families would have generally been treated in the same manner, when in fact the treatment of choice may have varied considerably with the type of family system.

One of the more promising attempts at the development of an approach to family assessment has been Olson, Russell and Sprenkle's (1983) development of a Family Adaptability and Cohesion Scale (FACES) that identifies families on a circumplex model according to family type and level of function or dysfunction. FACES is a 30 item self-report scale that provides an assessment of family cohesion and adaptability as perceived by each family member. The items assess nine concepts associated with cohesion and seven associated with adaptability. The Likert type response choices range from 1 (almost never) to 5 (almost always). Typical questions on the scale include:

Cohesion Dimension: "Family members are supportive of each other during difficult times." "In our family everyone goes his/her own way."

Adaptability Dimension: "It is hard to know what the rules are in our family." "We shift household responsibilities from person to person."

In developing this model, Olson conceptually clustered over 50 family research and therapy constructs and postulated two significant dimensions of family behavior: cohesion and adaptability. Cohesion was defined as the emotional bonding family members have with one another, and the degree of individual autonomy a member experiences within the family system. Adaptability is concerned with the ability of the family system to change its structure, role relationships and relationship rules in response to situational and developmental stress. Moderate levels of both cohesion and adaptability are presumed to be the most functional for family development. There is a need for a balance between too much closeness (enmeshed system), and too little closeness (disengaged system); and between too little change (rigid system), and too much change (chaotic system).

Specifically, families in the four central or balanced categories are assumed to function most effectively. Studies of parent-adolescent interaction have shown that high functioning families possess moderate levels of cohesion and adaptability whereas low functioning families present extreme levels on both dimensions (Druckman, 1979). She also noted that the juveniles in her study with the highest recidivism rates came from the extreme enmeshed category. This type of family would be characterized by extreme sensitivity of individual members to each other. Stress in one family member would be reflected in other family members and the behavior of one would immediately affect the others. The opposite of the enmeshed family is the disengaged family where family members are not noticeably aware of what is occurring with other family members. The famous Glueck studies (1950, 1962), reported a large number of these type of families (lack of cohesion), in the delinquent population that they studied. The circumplex model with location of families in the present study is depicted in Figure 1.

Purpose of Present Study

The primary purpose of this study was to further evaluate the clinical usefulness of the FACES instrument and the circumplex model with families referred to juvenile court intake. Other instruments developed by the authors and included in the assessment

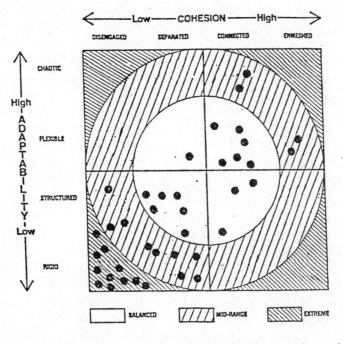

Figure 1. The Circumplex Model with location of sample families

strategy were designed to measure individual and family stress and parent-adolescent conflict.

It was postulated that there would be significant relationships between levels of stress in family members and level of family functioning (balanced, mid-range, and extreme) according to the circumplex. It was also hypothesized that parent-adolescent conflict would be more prevalent in the extreme families. Other variables of interest in the study included families' socioeconomic status, type of juvenile offense and how the sample FACES scores compared with national normative data.

RESULTS

The results presented is based on information obtained from 40 families and a total of 90 individuals residing in a medium-sized community in Southeast Missouri. The sample population was comprised of 40 juveniles referred to juvenile court intake and 50 parents who appeared with them. The ages of the youth in the study ranged from 10 to 16 with the average at 13.9 years. Sixty-seven percent of the juveniles were male ($n = 27$) and 33% were female ($n = 13$). The majority of the families were caucasian (72%) and the remainder of the families were black (28%). The study sample consisted of families referred during a nine-week period and although the sample was accidental and nonrandom, the court staff stated that the sample was representative of the typical cases referred.

Results from statistical analysis of data obtained with the FACES instrument revealed significant differences between the study sample and the national norms. The study sample were found to be significantly less cohesive and much more rigid than the national norms. The juveniles from the extreme families tended to commit more violent crimes (assault) or status offenses such as runaway, incorrigibility or truancy. The balanced and mid-range families were more likely to commit property crimes such as petty theft, minor vandalism or liquor related offenses such as buying beer with fake identification or underage possession of alcoholic beverages as indicated in Figure 2.

TYPE OF DELINQUENT ACT

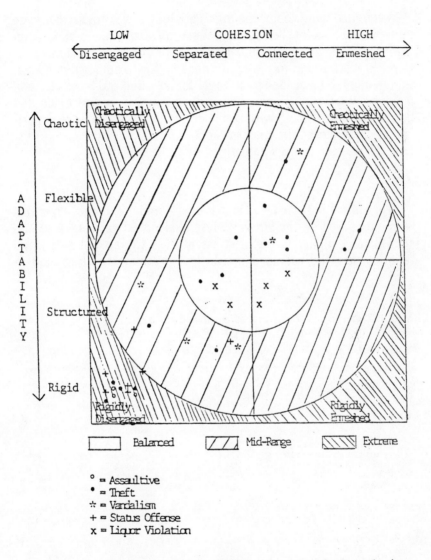

Figure 2. Type of Offense and Family Functioning

Socioeconomic Variables

When analyzing socioeconomic variables it was found that even though over 70% of the sample population was white, a significant majority of the extreme population was comprised of blacks. These families were found to have significantly less income, less education, tended to be headed by a single female, and had more children than the other two groups. An obvious conclusion was made that the families with the fewest socioeconomic resources were experiencing the greatest difficulty in functioning as a healthy family system. These results are summarized in Table 1.

Stress

When the "balanced," "mid-range," and "extreme" families were compared on the stress scales, analysis of variance revealed significantly higher levels of stress in the extreme and mid-range families than the balanced families as postulated as indicated in

Table 1

FAMILY SYSTEM CHARACTERISTICS
ACCORDING TO LEVEL OF FAMILY FUNCTIONING

Variable	Extreme		Mid-range		Balanced	
	N	%	N	%	N	%
Income						
Under $900	8	72.7	7	54.0	5	31.0
$900-$1200	3	27.3	2	15.0	5	31.0
Over $1200	0	---	4	31.0	6	38.0
Rent	10	91.0	6	46.0	6	38.0
Educational Level						
Non High School	8	72.7	5	38.4	7	44.0
High School Grad	3	27.3	6	46.2	3	19.0
Some College	0	---	2	15.4	4	25.0
Degree	0	---	0	---	2	12.0
Average Number of Children		3.4		2.9		2.6
Marital Status						
Single	6	55.0	3	23.0	3	18.8
Intact Family	3	27.0	6	46.0	8	50.0
Remarried	2	18.0	4	30.8	5	31.2
Race						
White	4	36.0	10	77.0	15	31.2
Black	7	64.0	3	23.0	1	6.0

Table 2. The most stressful items of adolescent and parents are presented in Tables 3 and 4.

Conflict

A comparison of the conflict scores between the three groups revealed no significant difference although a trend was clearly present. The extreme and mid-range families had higher mean scores than the balanced families. As indicated in Table 5 the mid-range families actually had the highest scores on the conflict scale.

It is postulated that the extreme disengagement that the families in the extreme categories feel for one another negates any conflict that they may be experiencing. They may be experiencing conflict, but the family members are not close enough to each other for the conflict to bother them as much as it does the closer-knit mid-range families.

Table 2

ANALYSIS OF VARIANCE OF STRESS
AND FAMILY FUNCTIONING

Groups	Adolescent Stress (ALEC) F-Score	Probability
Balanced & Mid-range X= 19.06 X= 32.38 n= 15 n= 16	12.68	p=<.001
Balanced & Extreme X= 19.06 X= 32.27 n= 15 n= 11	4.87	p=<.05
Mid-range & Extreme X= 32.38 X= 32.37 n= 16 n= 11	1.33	N.S.

Groups	Parent Stress (PLEC) F-Score	Probability
Balanced & Mid-range X= 16.72 X= 24.75 n= 18 n= 16	4.4	p=<.05
Balanced & Extreme X= 16.72 X= 27.6 n= 18 n= 13	8.70	p=<.01
Mid-range & Extreme X= 24.75 X= 27.6 n= 16 n= 13	1.08	N.S.

Table 3

MOST STRESSFUL ITEMS
PARENTS

Item	Frequency	%
Change in behavior of children	27	53.0
Change in arguments with child	22	43.2
Death of relative or close friend	21	41.0
Major illness or accident of relative	19	37.3
Threats of marital separation	18	35.3
Actual separation	14	27.5
Major illness or accident of close relative	14	27.5
Increase of unpaid bills	13	25.5
Personal injury of illness	11	21.6
Change in living conditions	11	21.6

Table 4

MOST STRESSFUL ITEMS
JUVENILES

Item	Frequency	%
Police arrest	25	62.5
Problems with police	23	57.5
School problems/bad grades	18	44.5
Arguments with parents	17	42.5
Physical threats or hits	15	37.5
Parents' conflict or violence	15	37.5
Use of alcohol	14	37.0
Relationship with opposite sex	14	35.0
Family money problems	12	30.0
Threats of being "sent off"	11	27.5

Table 5

PARENT-ADOLESCENT CONFLICT AND FAMILY FUNCTIONING

PAPC Response	Family Functioning			
	Balanced N = 34		Mid-R & Extreme N = 54	
	n	X	n	X
High Conflict	56	1.6	114	2.11
Some Conflict	276	8.7	641	11.87
Total Conflict	310	9.1	755	13.98

SUMMARY AND CONCLUSIONS

Juvenile and family courts across the country deal with multi-problemed families on a daily basis. They are in the unique position of being the primary screening agency for thousands of families who are experiencing problems with their juvenile court age children. Historically, juvenile courts have directed most of their resources in trying to solve the individual juvenile's problem rather than trying to help the entire family. Juvenile courts have generally not been successful due to the fact much of the juvenile's problems are the result of his family system and little is being done to help this system.

One of the questions most often asked by the juvenile court staff during the research was whether or not the battery of instruments would help determine which families needed the most help and which ones were basically normal. One of the purposes of this project was to develop such an assessment strategy that would have this type of practical significance. The results are promising and, at least for the sample population, the families at most risk were identified on several key variables. The circumplex model was found to be an excellent tool for diagnosing levels of family functioning and has great potential for widespread practical use in juvenile court settings. Utilizing FACES in conjunction with other instruments seems to be particularly beneficial in the establishment of a much needed "continuum of risk" assessment strategy.

Profiles of the "high risk" families identified in this study as compared to the "lower risk" family is presented in Table 6.

The prognosis for continued misbehavior of juveniles in the "high risk" family is postulated to be high without appropriate court intervention. Even then, family dysfunction is highly correlated to lack of socioeconomic resources and related stress which is difficult to change. In these cases formal adjudication and court monitoring combined with referral to appropriate community resources that may help with the economic problems would be warranted.

The "balanced families" on the other hand, were found to have significantly more economic resources and less stress than the high risk families and the juveniles seemed to commit offenses generally

Table 6

SAMPLE PROFILE OF HIGH VS LOW RISK FAMILIES
AS PROJECTED BY THE ASSESSMENT BATTERY

Balanced Families (low risk)	Extreme Families (high risk)
Income: over $1000.00 mo.	Income: under $900.00 mo.
Owns home	Rents home or apt.
High-school graduate	High-school dropout
Husband-wife dyad	Single female headed
Moderate to low family conflict	Moderate to high conflict
Moderate to low family stress	Moderate to high stress
2-3 children at home	3-4 children at home
Moderate to high family cohesiveness	Low family cohesiveness
Moderate to high family adaptability	Low family adaptability
Traditional delinquent act	More serious delinquent act or status offense

thought of as a "normal part of growing up." These appear to be relatively stable families with situational problems requiring minimal and unofficial court intervention.

The "mid-range" families in this study would seem to be the best prospects for short-term family intervention. They are experiencing high levels of conflict and stress possibly due to more transitional developmental problems than the chronic conditions that exist in the extreme families. These type of families might be excellent candidates for short-term (6 month) informal probation supervision coupled with appropriate family intervention as a prerequisite for dismissal.

It should be emphasized that this was an exploratory study and broad generalizations to other populations or for clinical intervention without further investigation is cautioned.

Suggestions for further research include testing and refining the model with larger and more diverse populations and longitudinal follow-up of "high risk" families utilizing the systemic assessment measures and recidivism rates.

REFERENCES

Aichorn, A., *Wayward Youth*. New York: Viking, 1935.
Baron, R., Feeny, F. & Thorton, W., Preventing delinquency through diversion: The Sacramento 601 diversion project. *Federal Probation*, 37, 13-18, 1973.

Druckman, J., A family oriented policy and treatment program for juvenile status offenders. *Journal of Marriage and the Family*, 3, 627-636, 1979.

Farrington, D.P. & West, D.J., The Familial Transmission of Crime. *Medical Science and Law*, 15, 177-186, 1975.

Glueck, S. & Glueck, E., *Unraveling juvenile delinquency*. Boston: Houghton Mifflin, 1962.

Goldstein, S., Brain research and violent behavior. *Archives of Neurology*, 30, 1-18, 1974.

Hutchison, J., *A comparative analysis of the costs of substitute care and family based services*. School of Social Work Monograph No. 2. Oaksdale, IA: University of Iowa, 1982.

Johnson, T.F., The result of family therapy with juvenile offenders. *Juvenile Justice*, 28, 29-33, 1977.

James, H., *Children in Trouble*. New York: David McKay, 1970.

Killorin, E. & Olson, D., The chaotic flippers in treatment. In E. Kaufman (ed.), *Power to change: Alcoholism*, Gardner Press, 1984.

Klein, N.C., Alexander, J.F. & Parsons, B.V., Impact of family systems intervention on recidivism and sibling delinquency: A model of primary prevention and program evaluation. *Journal of Consulting Clinical Psychology*, 45, 469-474, 1977.

McCord, J., Some child rearing antecedents to criminal behavior in adult men. *Journal of Personality and Social Psychology*, 27, 1477-1486, 1979.

McPherson, Mcdonald, L. & Ryer, C., Intensive counseling with families of juvenile offenders. *Juvenile and Family Court Journal*, 2, 32-33, 1983.

National Advisory Commission on Criminal Justice Standards and Goals, Juvenile Justice and Delinquency Prevention. Washington, DC: U.S. Government Printing Office, 1976.

Olson, D.H., Russell, C.S. & Sprenkle, D.H., Circumplex model of marital and family systems II. Empirical studies and clinical intervention. In John Vincent (ed.), *Advances in Family Intervention, Assessment and Theory*, Greenwich, CT: JAI Press, 1979.

Olson, D.H., Russell, C.S. & Sprenkle, D.H., Marital and family therapy: A decade review. *Journal of Marriage and Family*, 42, 973-993, 1980.

Olson, D.H., Russell, C.S. & Sprenkle, D.H., Circumplex model VI: Theoretical update. *Family Process*, 22, 3-28, 1983.

Pisciotto, A.W., Saving the Children: The promise and practice of Parens Patriae, 1938-98. *Crime and Delinquency*, 3, 411-412, 1982.

Presidents Commission on Law Enforcement and Administration of Justice: *Task Force on Juvenile Justice and Youth Crime*. Washington, DC: U.S. Government Printing Office, 1967.

Rowan, J., Parens Patriae is wrong: (Parent Supporter is Right). *Juvenile Justice*, 27, 17-23, 1976.

Smith, R. & Walters, J., Delinquent and non-delinquent perceptions of their fathers. *Adolescence*, 13, 21-28, 1978.

Stringfield, N., The impact of family counseling in resocializing adolescent offenders within a positive peer treatment milieu. *Journal of Offender Rehabilitation*, Spring, 1975.

Whitt, F. B., Family systems perspectives with juvenile delinquents, status offenders and dependent youth: An outcome and process evaluation of training. (Dissertation, Florida Institute of Technology, 1979). Dissertation Abstracts International, 40:2862B.

Wooden, K., *Weeping in the Playtime of Others*. New Jersey: National Coalition for Childrens Justice, 1977.

Glossary

Altruistic Suicide — Suicide which is selfless due to high integration into groups.

Anomic Suicide — Suicide which is due to normlessness (anomie); due to feelings of aimlessness or lack of clear cut directions.

Battered Woman Syndrome — Feelings of helplessness in the face of continued abuse including feelings of insecurity, dependency, nonassertiveness and self-deprecation.

Biological Positivism (in Criminology) — Theories which emphasized genetic determination of criminality.

Cambridge-Somerville Youth Study — A longitudinal study of delinquent youths conducted by the McCords.

Circumplex Model (of families) — A schema which identifies families according to type as well as level of function or dysfunction.

Classical Theory (in Criminology) — The belief that individuals exercise free will in hedonistically considering crime commission.

Complaint — A written statement or charge signed for or filed by a police officer in response to a domestic call.

Demonological Theory (in Criminology) — The belief that crime is caused by supernatural forces.

Deviant Behavior — A broad range of activities which society views as eccentric, dangerous, annoying, bizarre, outlandish, gross, abhorrent or criminal.

Differential Association Theory (in Criminology) — Sutherland's theory that individuals become predisposed toward criminality due to an excess of contacts which advocate criminal behavior.

Discriminant Analysis — A statistical procedure which permits the evaluation of the combined influence of a number of interval independent variables on an ordinal or nominal dependent variable.

Domestic Dispute — Any quarrel, altercation, or strife, including domestic violence between family or household members.

173

Domestic Violence — A domestic dispute in which a person or persons cause or attempt to cause physical harm to another family or household member.

Dualistic Fallacy — The mistaken assumption that criminals and noncriminals are mutually exclusive categories.

Durkheim's Theory of Suicide — Suicide is related to the strengths or weaknesses of group ties.

Ecological Fallacy — The error of drawing conclusions regarding individual behavior on the basis of data which have been derived from group or areal statistics.

Ecological theory (in Criminology) — The belief that group factors and characteristics impact upon crime commission.

Economic Theory (in Criminology) — Marxian belief that criminality is caused by economic conditions.

Egoistic Suicide — Self-centered suicide; due to low integration into group norms.

Exchange/Social Control theory (of family violence) — Gelles' theory that the family consists of various types of reciprocal "punishment and costs," and when members fail to honor their obligations others may retaliate.

FACES — A Family Adaptability and Cohesion Scale developed by Olson and his colleagues.

Fallacy of Autonomy — The belief that what goes on in the family is somehow separate from outside social forces that affect the family.

Family Systems Theory — A view of the family as an interrelated system which tends toward equilibrium or balance in which deviance on the part of a member is symptomatic of deeper, underlying disequilibrium within the system.

Freud's Psychodynamic Theory of Suicide — Suicide is a result of the need to relieve guilt which produces self-destructive attitudes and behavior.

Freud's Seduction Theory — Sexual abuse (missbrauch) in early childhood was the cause of adult hysteria.

Global Fallacy — The tendency to attempt to generalize relatively specific explanations to all types of crimes.

Guttman Scale — A procedure for developing a scale or index which is unidimensional (measures one dimension); a coefficient of reproducibility of .90 or higher is considered scalable or indicative of a successful scale.

Hedonism — The seeking of pleasure and avoidance of pain.

Homeostasis — Balance or equilibrium within a family system.

Isocracy — The reduction of the family to an aggregate of neutered, ageless, interchangeable members, bound together by contracts.

Love-Oriented Disciplinary Techniques — The use of positive discipline, e.g., praise and reasoning, or negative discipline, e.g., withdrawal of love, showing disappointment or isolation, in child rearing.

Lumpenproletariat — Marx's term for the dregs or underclass below the proletariat (workers).

Menninger's Theory of Suicide — Suicide is a composite death wish of wanting to kill, wanting to be killed, and wanting to die.

Parens Patriae — In juvenile treatment the state or court takes the position of parent in deciding the best interest of the child.

Parricide — The murder of parent/s by offspring.

Positivism — A scientific approach which emphasizes explaining and treating individual pathology.

Presenting Problem — A notion in family systems theory that crime or deviance is merely a symptom of deeper, more underlying disruption within the family system as a whole.

Psychological Positivism — Theories which concentrate upon the search for individual criminal pathology in the human personality.

Power-Oriented Disciplinary Techniques — The use of physical punishment, e.g., yelling, shouting and threatening, as a means of disciplining children.

Repressive (Institutionalized) Sublimation — Marcuse's term for the repression and channeling of sexuality through prescribed pathways of commerce and industry, while isolating the tender and erotic components which Freud posits as the basis of all civilized human relationships.

Rideout Case — A landmark court decision in which marital immunity was challenged as a defense for rape.

SES — An abbreviation for socioeconomic status; a composite measure of social class which includes income, education, occupation and other indicators.

Social Bonding — Tendency or desire to seek the company of a family member at the time when stress is being experienced.

Social Control Theories (in Criminology) — Approaches which hold that individuals have various containments or bonds which insulate them from social pressures.

Social Learning Theory (of family violence) — Early exposure to violence results in later violence as an adult.

Social Process Theories (in Criminology) — Theories which emphasize criminality as a learned or culturally transmitted process.

Subterranean Values — Underground or illicit values which exist side by side with more conventional ones.

Stress Theory (of intrafamily violence) — Family violence results when the natural defenses of persons are subject to high levels of stress and they are unable to cope.

Systems Theory (of families) — The family is viewed as similar to a living body having interrelated parts that support and complement each other's functions.

Techniques of Neutralization — Rationalization or means of explaining away responsibility for one's actions.

Tutelary Complex — Donzelot's concept that professional agencies have taken on much of the authority and socializing function of the family in exchange for a clean bill of family health.

Victimblaming — Gelles' notion that the victim of familial abuse blames himself for having incurred parental wrath and therefore deserved to be hit, or needed to be hit.

Violent Child Abuse — A practice involving the use of unlikely disciplinary instruments by an adult on a child; terror and the mere infliction of pain is viewed as the primary aim.